Letters *from the* Battlefront

The Civil War

VIRGINIA SCHOMP

BENCHMARK BOOKS

MARSHALL CAVENDISH

To Beth Schomp, our "steel magnolia"

Benchmark Books
Marshall Cavendish
99 White Plains Road
Tarrytown, New York 10591-9001
www.marshallcavendish.com

Text copyright © 2004 by Marshall Cavendish Corporation
Map © 2004 by Marshall Cavendish Corporation
Map by Laszlo Kubinyi

Library of Congress Cataloging-in-Publication Data

Schomp, Virginia.
The Civil War / by Virginia Schomp.
p. cm. — (Letters from the battlefront)
Summary: Describes the Civil War through the letters of the people who
fought it on both sides, including the voices of women on the front and
the experiences of African Americans.
Includes bibliographical references (p.) and index.
ISBN 0-7614-1660-9
1. United States—History—Civil War, 1861-1865—Personal
narratives—Juvenile literature. 2. United States—History—Civil War,
1861-1865—African Americans—Juvenile literature. 3. United
States—History—Civil War, 1861-1865—Women—Juvenile literature. [1.
United States—History—Civil War, 1861-1865. 2. United
States—History—Civil War, 1861-1865—Personal narratives.] I. Title
II. Series: Schomp, Virginia. Letters from the battlefront.

E464.S36 2003
973.7'8—dc21   2003009855

Book design by Patrice Sheridan
Art Research: Rose Corbett Gordon, Mystic CT
Cover: SuperStock
Bettmann/Corbis: page 14; Corbis: pages 37 & 67; Geoffrey Clements/Corbis; page 25; The Granger Collection,
New York: pages 9, 19, 21, 30, 35, 39, 41, 48, 52, 54, 55, 59, 62, 68, 74, & 77; Hulton Archive/Getty Images: pages 17 & 51;
New-York Historical Society /Bridgeman Art Library: page 11; North Wind Picture Archives: page 43; Pennsylvania
State Archives: page 72.
Printed in China
1 3 5 6 4 2

A Note on Editing

In order to preserve the "personality" and historic accuracy of the letters and other writings in this book, we have done as little editing as possible. Many people in Civil War times did not follow any standard rules for spelling, capitalization, or punctuation, but in most cases we have not modernized the resulting oddities of style. We have occasionally added words in brackets to make meanings clear. Ellipses (. . .) show where words have been dropped.

Contents

From the Author

Letters from the Battlefront is written as a companion to the *Letters from the Homefront* series. The books in that series told the story of America's wars from the viewpoint of those who worked, watched, and waited at home. These books look at the same conflicts through the eyes of the men and women on the front lines.

Historians often study letters and journals written by famous people—explorers, philosophers, kings—to gain information about the past. Recently they have discovered the value of writings by "ordinary" people, too. Students of history have begun to seek out and study the personal writings of farmers and merchants, slaves and slaveholders, sailors and foot soldiers. Documents such as these, often called primary sources, help us to understand the beliefs, hopes, and dreams of earlier generations and to learn how historical events shaped their lives.

This book uses primary sources to recapture the drama of life during the Civil War. In these pages you will hear the words of Northerners and Southerners who fought for very different ideas of liberty, honor, and country. You will meet the African Americans who turned the struggle to save the Union into a fight for freedom. You will read about women who stepped out of their traditional roles to work and fight on the battlefront. It is a story told in their own words, in their letters, diaries, and personal reflections on the momentous conflict that destroyed slavery and redefined the United States as a nation.

Introduction

America Divided

On the eve of the Civil War, the United States seemed like *two* nations. The North was a land of growth and prosperity. By 1860, it had more than 100,000 factories and its railroads stretched 20,000 miles—more than the rest of the world's rails combined. About one-third of the Northern population of 22 million people lived in large cities or towns. In contrast, the South had a population of only 9 million, less than 20,000 factories, and 9,000 miles of railways. The overwhelming majority of Southerners lived and worked on farms.

The wide gap between North and South led to many disagreements over politics, laws, and trade. But the most important conflict centered on the issue of slavery.

Slavery in America dated back to the earliest permanent English settlement. The first slaves, a group of twenty people, were brought from Africa to Jamestown, Virginia, in 1619. Hundreds of thousands followed. Slavery gradually died out in the North, because it proved impractical in the region's factories and small farms. In the South, however, a large, cheap slave labor force became the foundation of an economy built on plantations—huge farms where cotton, tobacco, and other crops were grown. In 1860 there were four million American slaves, and nine out of ten of them labored in Southern farm fields.

Abolitionists called for an end to slavery. Southerners, who already felt threatened by the North's growing wealth and power, protested this interference with

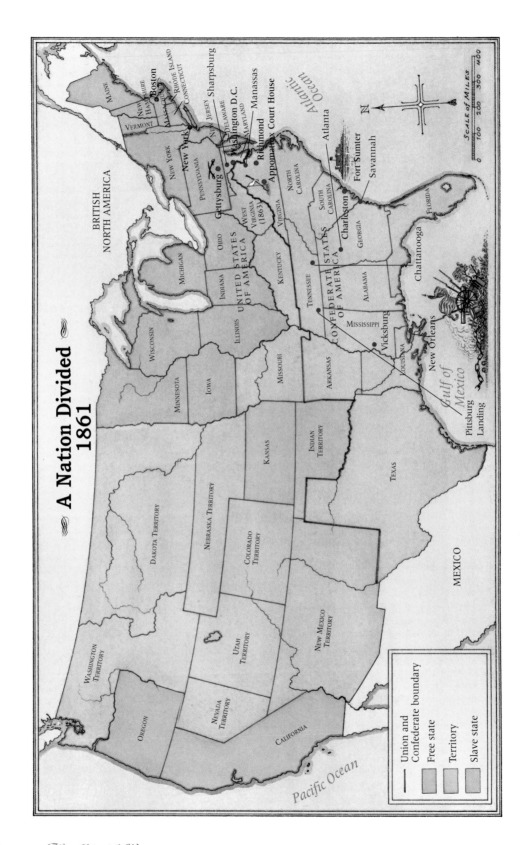

A Nation Divided
1861

BRITISH NORTH AMERICA

Legend:
- Union and Confederate boundary
- Free state
- Territory
- Slave state

States and Territories: MAINE, VERMONT, NEW HAMPSHIRE, MASSACHUSETTS, RHODE ISLAND, CONNECTICUT, NEW YORK, NEW JERSEY, PENNSYLVANIA, DELAWARE, MARYLAND, OHIO, INDIANA, ILLINOIS, MICHIGAN, WISCONSIN, MINNESOTA, IOWA, MISSOURI, KENTUCKY, WEST VIRGINIA (1863), VIRGINIA, NORTH CAROLINA, SOUTH CAROLINA, GEORGIA, FLORIDA, TENNESSEE, ALABAMA, MISSISSIPPI, LOUISIANA, ARKANSAS, TEXAS, KANSAS, DAKOTA TERRITORY, NEBRASKA TERRITORY, COLORADO TERRITORY, INDIAN TERRITORY, NEW MEXICO TERRITORY, UTAH TERRITORY, NEVADA TERRITORY, WASHINGTON TERRITORY, OREGON, CALIFORNIA, MEXICO

Places: Boston, Sharpsburg, Washington D.C., Manassas, Appomattox Court House, Gettysburg, Richmond, Atlanta, Fort Sumter, Savannah, Charleston, Chattanooga, Vicksburg, New Orleans, Pittsburg Landing

UNITED STATES OF AMERICA

CONFEDERATE STATES OF AMERICA

Atlantic Ocean

Gulf of Mexico

Pacific Ocean

Scale of Miles: 0 100 200 300 400

N

their economy and way of life. The debate grew increasingly bitter as the country expanded west and Americans argued over whether slavery should be allowed to spread with it. Throughout the 1840s and 1850s, pro- and antislavery politicians worked out compromises, admitting some Western territories into the Union as free states, some as slave states. Still, resentments simmered, sometimes erupting into violence. One of the most divisive incidents occurred in October 1859, when abolitionist John Brown and a small band of followers raided the federal arsenal at Harpers Ferry, Virginia, in an attempt to seize weapons and start a slave uprising. Seventeen people were killed in the failed attack. Brown was captured and hanged for treason. Northerners praised him as a martyr to the antislavery cause, and outraged Southerners became convinced there could be "no peace for the South in the Union."

Radical Southerners had already begun talking about secession (withdrawal from the Union). Now, as the crisis over slavery and the hostilities between North and South deepened, many moderates joined the secessionist movement. During the presidential campaign of 1860, secessionists strongly opposed the Republican candidate, Abraham Lincoln. Lincoln was a moderate who pledged to leave slavery alone where it existed but to halt its further spread. He won the presidency with just 40 percent of the popular vote, carrying most Northern states but not a single state in the South. To prideful Southerners, his election was a "declaration of war against our property and the supremacy of the white race." In December 1860 South Carolina seceded from the Union. Within a month and a half, six other Southern states had followed, forming an independent nation, the Confederate States of America.

In his inaugural address in March 1861, President Lincoln vowed to preserve the Union and protect U.S. government property. On April 12 the Confederates responded by attacking and capturing Fort Sumter in South Carolina. Lincoln called for 75,000 volunteer soldiers to suppress the rebellion, and four more Southern states took up arms for the Confederacy. The bloodiest war in U.S. history had begun. For the next four years, Americans would fight and kill Americans in a deadly struggle over the future of the nation and the meaning of freedom.

One

Fighting for the Confederacy

The Yankees are a blue-bellied, green-backed, yellow-eyed, brown-footed, black-hearted and white-livered set. Such a combination of colors is bound to run.

—A CONFEDERATE SOLDIER

"The Holy Cause"

Southerners responded to the coming of war with noisy enthusiasm and optimism. "I never in my life witnessed such excitement," said one Virginian in the new Confederate capital at Richmond. Everyone was "perfectly frantic with delight."

When Confederate President Jefferson Davis called for 100,000 volunteers to form a Southern army, young men raced to enlist. Farmers abandoned their plows and merchants "dropped their ledgers." Colleges suspended classes for lack of students. All were certain that "the scum of the North" would topple after one good fight.

This proud, defiant young Southerner is wearing the full-dress uniform of a Confederate fighting man.

IN FEBRUARY 1861 FORMER MISSISSIPPI SENATOR JEFFERSON DAVIS WAS ELECTED PRESIDENT OF THE NEWLY FORMED CONFEDERATE STATES OF AMERICA. WHILE MOST SOUTHERNERS WERE OPTIMISTIC ABOUT THEIR CHANCES IN A WAR AGAINST THE NORTH, DAVIS KNEW THAT HE FACED A MONUMENTAL TASK. IN HIS FIRST LETTER TO HIS WIFE, VARINA, AFTER HIS INAUGURATION, THE PRESIDENT SHARED HIS CONCERNS FOR HIS NEW NATION. DAVIS WROTE FROM MONTGOMERY, ALABAMA, WHICH WAS THE CENTER OF THE CONFEDERATE GOVERNMENT UNTIL MAY 1861, WHEN VIRGINIA SECEDED AND THE CAPITAL WAS MOVED TO RICHMOND.

Montgomery, Ala., February 20, 1861

My dear Wife,

I have been so crowded and pressed that the first wish to write to you has been thus long deferred [delayed].

I was inaugurated on Monday, having reached here on Saturday night. The audience was large and brilliant. Upon my weary heart was showered smiles, plaudits [praise], and flowers; but, beyond them, I saw troubles and thorns innumerable.

We are without machinery, without means, and threatened by a powerful opposition; but I do not despond, and will not shrink from the task imposed upon me.

All along the route, except when in Tennessee, the people at every station manifested good-will and approbation by bonfires at night, firing by day; shouts and salutations in both.

I thought it would have gratified you to have witnessed it, and have been a memory to our children.

Thus I constantly wish to have you all with me.—Here I was interrupted by the Secretary of the Congress, who brought me two bills to be approved. This is a gay and handsome town of some eight thousand inhabitants, and will not be an unpleasant residence. As soon as an hour is my own, I will look for a house and write to you more fully.

Devoted love to you and the children,

Your husband

Much of the Confederates' confidence came from faith in the justice of their cause. Southern men volunteered from a mixture of motives: a sense of honor and duty, the desire for adventure, pressure from friends and community. But overrid-

A wealthy Southerner and his human "property." At the beginning of the Civil War, one out of every seven Americans belonged to another.

ing all was their belief in what one enlisted man called "the holy cause of Southern freedom."

Like the Patriots of the American Revolution, Confederate soldiers pledged to defend their country against the "tyrants" who threatened their homes, property, and independence. Only about one-third of the men came from slaveholding families, but all opposed Yankee interference with the right to own human "property." They saw no contradiction in fighting for both slavery and freedom. "If we should suffer ourselves to be subjugated by the tyrannical government of the North," wrote one Virginian, "our property would all be confiscated . . . & our people reduced to the most abject bondage." To this Southerner and many thousands like him, the only honorable course was to "respond to the language of the great Patrick Henry in the days of '76 & say give me Liberty or give me death."

In the Confederate Camp

Despite their eagerness for action, most Confederates would have to wait long weeks or months before facing the enemy. First, volunteer companies must be formed and filled up. Then the recruits had to be outfitted with uniforms, battle flags, weapons, and ammunition, often crafted by patriotic local women's groups and blacksmiths. Finally, the men set off for army camps, with colors flying and fifes and drums sounding. Sam Watkins, a private with the First Tennessee Regiment, was thrilled by the reception his regiment received along its train ride to Virginia.

> We went bowling along . . . thirty miles an hour, as fast as steam could carry us. At every town and station, citizens and ladies were waving their handkerchiefs and hurrahing for Jeff Davis and the Southern Confederacy. . . . Ah, it is worth soldiering to receive such welcomes as this.

Life in an army camp proved far less exciting. Drilling for hours a day was hard work, and performing guard duty when the nearest Yankee was miles away didn't seem much like soldiering. When the recruits weren't drilling or standing guard, they chopped wood, toted water, prepared food, washed clothes, and cleaned the camp. For entertainment they played cards, attended prayer meetings, read books and newspapers, and wrote letters home. Long stretches of boredom led to arguments and fistfights. Company officers, who were elected by the men themselves, had a hard time imposing discipline. The independence-minded volunteers questioned orders, left camp without leave, skipped drill in bad weather, and shirked boring chores. "Made my first detail . . . for guard duty," wrote a Mississippi sergeant in May 1861, "to which most men objected because they said they did not enlist to do guard duty but to fight the Yankees—all fun and frolic."

By the end of the year, most Confederates had outgrown the notion that war was fun. Although they would never be as disciplined or well trained as soldiers in modern American armies, most had learned the value of order and obedience to authority. Some had already seen battle. All would have their ideals of patriotism, honor, and duty tested in the hard months and years ahead.

WINTER WAS A TIME OF EXTREME DISCOMFORT, INACTION, AND BOREDOM FOR THE ARMIES OF BOTH NORTH AND SOUTH. SIDNEY LANIER OF GEORGIA, STATIONED IN VIRGINIA DURING THE WINTER OF 1861 TO 1862, SENT THIS LETTER TO HIS BROTHER, CLIFF, DESCRIBING WINTER'S TRIALS AND HOW ONE GROUP OF CONFEDERATES MANAGED TO ESCAPE THEM.

[December 1861]

You would not think, my dear Cliff, that I was a soldier, enduring the frowns of "grim-visaged [grim-faced] war," if you could see me with slippers and smoking-cap on, pipe in mouth, writing to you on a real pine table, surrounded by ten noisy boys, in a room with ten sleeping-bunks built against its walls, and a "great and glorious" fire blazing in the fireplace—I can hardly realize that I am in a house, but find myself continually asking myself if it is not some delightful dream; it is impossible for you to realize with what delight I hail a real, bona-fide room as a habitation for the winter, unless you had, as I have, shivered in cold tents for the last few months . . . ; unless you had become accustomed, 1st, to going to sleep with the expectation that your tent would blow down and the rains wet you to the skin before you could get your clothes on; and, 2nd, to having the said expectations realized in the most satisfactory manner; unless you had been in the habit of eating in a drenching rain which diluted your coffee (without any sugar) before you could drink it, and made mush of your biscuit before you could eat it; . . . unless you had, in short, been as horribly uncomfortable as it is possible for a man to be.—The room, which so excites my delight, is the one which my mess [group] occupies in our winter-quarters, which we have been actively engaged in building for two weeks past. . . .

It is rumored in camp that our Battalion may possibly be discharged [released from duty] in January, tho' I am not disposed to attach much importance to the rumor. . . .

I think it extremely probable that we will have peace in the Spring.

Sidney Lanier was a volunteer in the Georgia Infantry and later served aboard a Confederate blockade runner. After the war he became a well-known poet and musician.

Early Southern Victories

The first big battle of the Civil War took place beside a stream called Bull Run, near the town of Manassas Junction, Virginia.* About 35,000 Confederates under General Pierre Beauregard were gathered near Manassas, menacing Washington, D.C., to the north and protecting Richmond to the south. On July 21, 1861, 37,000 Union troops under General Irvin McDowell advanced on the town, planning to crush the rebellion with one mighty blow. Hundreds of civilians and politicians rode out from Washington with picnic baskets and binoculars to enjoy the show.

At first, the Yankees beat back the Confederates. As a Massachusetts private recalled, "The boys were saying constantly, in great glee, 'We've whipped them.' 'We'll hang Jeff Davis to a sour apple tree.' 'They are running.'" But late in the afternoon, after hours of fierce fighting, Confederate General Thomas "Stonewall" Jackson led a sudden massive counterattack, urging his men to "yell like furies!" The Union troops fell back, only to find their way blocked by the carriages of the civilian spectators. Their orderly retreat became a rout. Panicky Yankees threw down their packs and weapons, pushing and shoving to escape the battlefield. Then the whole noisy, tangled mass of soldiers, civilians, horses, and wagons surged down the road back to Washington.

The First Battle of Bull Run was a stunning victory for the Confederacy. Southerners gloated over the Union's humiliation and proclaimed the war as good as won. Some Confederate soldiers even left the army and returned to their homes and businesses. But the disastrous defeat had only roused the North. After Bull Run President Lincoln called for a half million more volunteers, and the Union geared up for a long, costly fight.

Rich Man's War, Poor Man's Fight

Southern spirits remained high through the end of 1861, boosted by Confederate victories in battles at Wilson's Creek, Missouri, and Leesburg, Virginia. By the

*The North usually named battles for bodies of water or other land features, the South for the nearest town. So for Northerners, this was the First Battle of Bull Run; for Southerners, the First Battle of Manassas.

spring of 1862, however, confidence had begun to crumble. The bloody carnage of the Battle of Shiloh, fought at Pittsburg Landing, Tennessee, on April 6 and 7, shocked both North and South. After the first day of that battle, the rebels were convinced "those Yankees were whipped, fairly whipped." The tide turned when Union reinforcements arrived, forcing the Confederates to withdraw. Shiloh claimed some 23,000 dead, wounded, or missing. More men died than in all previous American wars combined.

Soon after Shiloh the Union navy captured New Orleans, the South's most important Mississippi River port. The Yankees seemed poised to gobble up the whole Mississippi Valley as well as the entire West. And just as the Confederate cause faltered, its forces were beginning to shrink. Rebel soldiers were sick of the hardships of army life. Many planned to go home when their twelve-month enlistments expired, and there weren't enough new volunteers to take their place.

The Rebel Yell

Yankee soldiers at Bull Run were the first to hear the "rebel yell." No one knows exactly what this Confederate battle cry sounded like. One historian believes it was "a sort of fox-hunt yip mixed up with a sort of banshee squall."

Rebels let loose their famous yell when they charged enemy positions. When it was first used, the cry was probably a natural release of fear, tension, and hatred. After Confederate officers saw its terrifying effect on the enemy, they began to urge their men to yell with every charge. Years after the war one Union veteran swore that there was nothing like the rebel yell "this side of the infernal region. The peculiar corkscrew sensation that it sends down your backbone . . . can never be told. You had to feel it, and if you say you did not feel it, and heard the yell, you have *never* been there."

Three Confederate soldiers captured in battle await shipment to a Union prisoner-of-war camp.

On April 16, 1862, the Confederate Congress responded to the crisis by passing the first conscription law, or draft law, in American history. Every able-bodied white man between the ages of eighteen and thirty-five was required to serve in the army for three years. "A more oppressive law was never enacted in the most uncivilized country," protested one soldier from South Carolina. "The Conscript Act will do away with all the patriotism we have." Most infuriating of all, the law allowed well-to-do Southerners to hire substitutes to serve in their place and completely exempted men who owned twenty slaves or more. "This is a Rich mans Woar," wrote a bitter North Carolina man, "but the poor man has to do the fiting."

MANY CONFEDERATE SOLDIERS GREW WEARY OF WAR AS THEY BEGAN TO REALIZE THAT THE YANKEES WOULD NOT BE SO EASY TO BEAT. ESPECIALLY EAGER TO RETURN HOME WERE NON-SLAVEHOLDING FARMERS WHO HAD LEFT A WIFE AND SMALL CHILDREN BEHIND, LIKE LUKE ROBERTS OF ALABAMA. A FEW WEEKS AFTER LUKE SENT THIS LETTER TO HIS WIFE, CASSEA, AND THEIR FIVE CHILDREN, THE CONSCRIPTION ACT EXTENDED HIS TERM OF SERVICE TO THREE YEARS. HE WAS KILLED IN ACTION AT PORT GIBSON, MISSISSIPPI, IN MAY 1863.

Camp Jobe Kerry, Near Taladega, Ala., March 28th, 1862

Mrs. C. M. Roberts,
Madam,

I am doing very well only I want to see you very bad, but I dont want to come till I get my money. I expect it will be tolerably soon. . . .

I received your kind letter and was forced to shed tears to look upon the beautiful handwriting of our daughter (Josie) and her kind letter to me. She stated to me that Henry would go to the door and call for dady. May God bless his little mouth, dady wishes he could be there with him to answer to his sweet calls and hear him jabber. Tell Aaron and Nathan they must be good boys, that dady was glad to hear that they would mind what their mamma would tell them and dady will try to come home and bring them some little money. Emely and Josie, keep practicing reading and writing and learn Aaron and Nathan all you can. Emely you write almost too fast, if you will take your time and be careful and not leave out any words nor letters you will write a nice hand.

We have prayer meeting every night in camp. We have a little methodist preacher by the name of Lucus. Some nights he has as many as twelve mourners [worshippers] I believe to be in good earnest while some others is not. This is the wickedest place that I ever was in in my life. I cant help but get on my knees and implore the mercies of God on our encampment and on our entire country, and especially for my family and friends. I have none other to put my trust in than God who is able to aid in time of need. May God bless you all is my prayer. . . .

Luke R. Roberts

Bloody Day at Antietam

The summer of 1862 brought renewed hopes for the Confederacy. Thanks to fumbling military leadership in the North, the Union war effort had fizzled out. Meanwhile, the bold and decisive General Robert E. Lee had taken command of the Confederate Army of Northern Virginia. In August Lee launched a surprise attack on Union forces at Manassas Junction, the site of the North's defeat a year earlier. The Second Battle of Bull Run ended in another decisive Confederate victory, driving most of the Northern army out of the South.

In September Lee took his army across the Potomac River, intending to capture the Union railroad center at Harrisburg, Pennsylvania. His men never made it that

Union troops charge Confederate positions near a small, white church at the Battle of Antietam, September 17, 1862. One Southern soldier recalled that "the sunbeams falling on their well-polished guns and bayonets gave a glamour and a show at once fearful and entrancing."

far. By chance, a Yankee soldier stumbled across a copy of the general's battle orders, which had been dropped in a field by a careless messenger. The plans contained vital information on how the Confederates had divided their troops and where each branch of their army was headed. Learning of the breach in security, Lee raced to bring his scattered forces together in the small town of Sharpsburg, Maryland, by a creek called Antietam.

The Yankees attacked at dawn on September 17. For twelve hours savage fighting surged back and forth across a landscape of woods, farm fields, and country lanes. Near a small white church, rebel fire cut down two thousand Union soldiers in twenty minutes. In another corner of the battlefield, Confederates in a narrow sunken road held off charge after charge, until the Yankees finally broke through and shot them "like sheep in a pen." Beyond a big cornfield rebels fell under Union artillery that cut "every stalk of corn . . . as closely as could have been done with a knife. . . . The slain lay in rows precisely as they had stood in their ranks a few moments before."

Twenty-three thousand men were killed or wounded at Antietam, on the bloodiest single day of the war. Those losses included one-quarter of Lee's army. Outnumbered and worn out, the Confederates retreated back across the Potomac.

"Almost Starved Out"

Through the winter of 1862–1863, the North rebuilt and resupplied its armies. The South struggled to do the same, but against far greater odds. With its smaller population and manufacturing capabilities, the Confederacy was suffering growing shortages of manpower and military equipment. The Union navy blockaded Confederate ports, cutting off imports of badly needed supplies as well as exports of cash-producing cotton. Southern farm fields produced bountiful crops, but the poor railroad system made it nearly impossible to deliver food and other supplies to the army. In September 1862 one Confederate soldier wrote in his diary, "Our army is . . . almost starved out. Our rations has been Beef and flour since we left Richmond and not more than half enough of that[. Many] times we had Green Corn and apples issued to us and were glad to get that."

Despite all their hardships Southerners continued their resistance. At the close of 1862, the rebel army soundly thrashed the Yankees at Fredericksburg, Virginia.

In May 1863 it defeated a Union force nearly twice its size at nearby Chancellorsville. The brilliant victory at Chancellorsville came at a great cost: nearly 13,000 Confederate casualties. Among those killed was Lee's most valued commander, Stonewall Jackson, who was accidentally shot down by his own troops.

The Battle of Gettysburg

After Chancellorsville Robert E. Lee led his army on a second Northern invasion. The Confederate general hoped the offensive would relieve pressures in the West, where Union forces under General Ulysses S. Grant held the vital city of Vicksburg, Mississippi, under siege. Lee also hoped that a decisive victory on Northern soil would win recognition and aid for the Confederacy from European powers. Most importantly, such a victory might shake up the Union, rouse Northern antiwar forces, and bring the war to a close.

On July 1, 1863, advance units of Lee's army ran into a detachment of Union cavalry in southern Pennsylvania. Shots rang out, and both sides sent for reinforcements. Soon 85,000 Yankees and 65,000 Confederates converged on the small country town of Gettysburg.

The Yankees quickly secured the hilltops overlooking the town. Lee was convinced that

General Robert E. Lee, commander of the Army of Northern Virginia. Lee's second invasion of the North ended in defeat at the Battle of Gettysburg in July 1863.

his troops could capture the high ground and crush the Union army. For two days the Confederates made wave after wave of brave assaults. Each time they were beaten back by the equally courageous defenders. "The edge of the conflict surged to and fro," said a Union private stationed on a hill called Little Round Top, "with wild whirlpools and eddies. At times I saw around me more of the enemy than of my own men." One Texan who fought to capture the hill recalled that "the balls were whizzing so thick that it looked like a man could hold out a hat and catch it full."

On July 3 General Lee ordered fellow Virginian George E. Pickett to attack the center of the Union position, on Cemetery Hill. The Confederates had to charge across nearly a mile of open fields. Union artillery and rifle fire mowed them down by the thousands. The few rebels who reached the Union line faced "bayonet thrusts, sabre strokes, pistol shots. . . . Men [fell] down on their hands and knees, spinning round like tops, throwing out their arms, gulping blood, falling." Many of the survivors of Pickett's Charge threw down their weapons and surrendered.

OUT OF THE 13,000 REBEL SOLDIERS WHO TOOK PART IN PICKETT'S CHARGE, SOME 6,500 WERE KILLED, WOUNDED, OR CAPTURED. THE DISASTROUS ASSAULT ENDED THE BATTLE OF GETTYSBURG. THREE DAYS AFTER THE CONFEDERATE DEFEAT, GENERAL PICKETT, STILL SICKENED WITH HORROR AND GUILT, WROTE TO HIS FIANCÉE, LA SALLE CORBELL.

Headquarters, July 6, 1863

On the Fourth—far from a glorious Fourth to us or to any with love for his fellow-men— I wrote you just a line of heart-break. The sacrifice of life on that blood-soaked field on the fatal third was too awful for the heralding of victory, even for our victorious foe, who, I think, believe as we do, that it decided the fate of our cause. No words can picture the anguish of that roll-call—the breathless waits between the responses. The "Here" of those who, by God's mercy, had miraculously escaped the awful rain of shots and shell was a sob—a gasp—a knell [bell toll]—for the unanswered name of his comrade called before his. There was no tone of thankfulness for having been spared to answer to their names, but rather a toll, and an unvoiced wish that they, too, had been among the missing.

But for the blight to your sweet young life, but for you, only you, my darling, your soldier would rather by far be out there, too, with his brave Virginians—dead—

Even now I can hear them cheering as I gave the order, "Forward"! I can feel their faith and trust in me and their love for our cause. I can feel the thrill of their joyous voices as they called out all along the line, "We'll follow you, Marse George. We'll follow you—we'll follow you." Oh, how faithfully they kept their word—following me on—on—to their death, and I, believing in the promised support, led them on—on—on—Oh, God!

I can't write you a love letter to-day, my Sallie, for with my great love for you and my gratitude to God for sparing my life to devote to you, comes the over-powering thought of those whose lives were sacrificed—of the broken-hearted widows and mothers and orphans. The moans of my wounded boys, the sight of the dead, upturned faces, flood my soul with grief—and here am I whom they trusted, whom they followed, leaving them on that field of carnage. . . .

Your
Soldier

The Battle of Gettysburg cost the South 28,000 men—more than one-third of its army. On July 4 Lee's battered troops retreated. As they limped back toward Virginia, news arrived of another disaster: the besieged Confederate forces at Vicksburg had surrendered. "Many of us shed tears at the way in which our dreams of liberty had ended," recalled Napier Bartlett of Louisiana, "and then and there gave them a much more careful burial than most of the dead received."

Two

All for the Union

The soldiers' fare is very rough,
The bread is hard, the beef is tough;
If they can stand it, it will be,
Through love of God, a mystery.

—A YANKEE SOLDIER, APRIL 1863

Yankees to War

"War! and volunteers are the only topics of conversation or thought," wrote an Ohio college student a week after the fall of Fort Sumter. "The lessons today have been a mere form. I cannot study. I cannot sleep, I cannot work, and I dont know as I can write."

Like their cousins down south, Northerners were swept up in a surge of patriotism and excitement as the Civil War began. More than a hundred thousand men joined the Union army in the early weeks of the war. They came for glory and adventure, for steady work and pay, for love of country and hatred of the rebels who threatened to destroy it. And, like the Confederates, Yankees believed they were fighting for the ideals of the American Revolution. "Thousands went forth and poured out their lifs blood in the Revolution to establish this government," wrote one young Northern volunteer, "and twould be a disgrace to the whole American people if she had not noble sons enough who had the spirit of seventy six in their hearts."

Drummers and buglers sounded daily calls at Union army camps. Their calls announced break-fast and dinner, assembly, company drill, and other duties and routines.

PATRIOTISM WAS ESPECIALLY STRONG AMONG THE THOUSANDS OF IMMIGRANTS WHO ENLIST-ED IN THE UNION ARMY. MANY OF THESE MEN HAD COME TO THE UNITED STATES TO ESCAPE POVERTY AND OPPRESSION AT HOME, AND THEY SAW THE UNION AS A SYMBOL OF HOPE AND FREEDOM. IRISH-BORN CARPENTER PETER WELSH JOINED THE 28TH MASSACHUSETTS INFANTRY IN THE SUMMER OF 1862. HIS WIFE, MARGARET, STRONGLY OPPOSED HIS ENLIST-MENT, AND HE SENT HER A NUMBER OF LETTERS EXPLAINING HIS DEVOTION TO THE UNION CAUSE. MARGARET'S WORST FEARS WERE REALIZED IN MAY 1864, WHEN PETER WAS FATALLY WOUNDED DURING THE BATTLE OF SPOTSYLVANIA, VIRGINIA.

February the 3d/63

My dear wife
. . . i know that it is hard for you and that you must feel lonesome and it is also hard for me to be so long seperated from you . . . But now my dear wife if you will just come with me a few moments into the merits of the case we will see on what grounds we stand   In the first place rebellion without a just cause is a crime of the greatest magnitude . . . you may say what is it to me   let them fight it out between themselves   this i know is said by many but who are they!   this is my country as much as the man that was born on the soil and so it is with every man who comes to this country and becomes a citezen   this being the case i have as much interest in the maintenance of the goverment and laws and the integrity of the nation as any other man   this war with all its evils with all its erors and missmanagement is a war in which the people of all nations have a vital interest   this is the first test of a modern free government in the act of sustaining itself against internal enemys and matured rebellion   all men who love free government and equal laws are watching this crisis to see if a republic can sustain itself in such a case   if it fail then the hopes of milions fall and the desighns and wishes of all tyrants will suceed   how many thousands are there in this country who saw nothing but opression and mis-ery at home who are now in comfort . . . Contrast the conditions of the masses of this with any other country in the world and the advantages we enjoy will stand out boldly so that the blindest can see them . . . Here the poorest . . . takes his start with all the honours and the hiest position that a great nation can bestow open before him. . . .

Your loving husband
Peter Welsh

Few white Northerners fought for the abolition of slavery. Although they owned no slaves, most were deeply prejudiced against blacks. Like Simeon Norton of Connecticut, they believed that the "Union never could have been formed without tolerating slavery, and . . . never can be restored without guaranteeing it."

As they traveled through the South, many Union soldiers found their point of view changing. Some blamed slavery for what they saw as Southern backwardness and ignorance. Some were horrified by their first up-close look at the "accursed institution." Many began to believe that the war would never end without the emancipation of the slaves. "I believe that Slavery . . . was the sole cause of this Rebellion," wrote an Iowa private in January 1862, "and untill this cause is removed and slavery abolished, the rebellion will continue."

In September 1862 Abraham Lincoln issued the Emancipation Proclamation, freeing all slaves in the Confederate states. A majority of Union soldiers approved the move, but thousands felt betrayed. John Ford of Kentucky argued that the men in his regiment had "volunteered to fight to restore the Old Constitution and not to free the Negroes . . . and we are not a-going to do it." In time, however, even hard-core foes of abolition often changed their minds, for purely practical reasons. "I have always untill lately been opposed to abraham linkins proclamation," wrote a Pennsylvania private in 1863, "but i have lately been convinced that it was just the thing that was neded to weaken the strength of the rebls."

HISTORIANS ESTIMATE THAT FEWER THAN ONE IN TEN SOLDIERS FOUGHT FOR THE UNION WITH THE GOAL OF ENDING SLAVERY. AMONG THAT MINORITY WAS FUTURE U.S. PRESIDENT JAMES A. GARFIELD. A COMMITTED ABOLITIONIST, GARFIELD ENLISTED AS A LIEUTENANT-COLONEL IN THE 42ND OHIO INFANTRY IN AUGUST 1861. IN THIS LETTER TO HIS WIFE, LUCRETIA, HE DESCRIBED HIS IMPRESSIONS OF SLAVERY IN THE DEEP SOUTH.

Tuscumbia, Alabama
June 14, 1862

My Dear Crete:
We reached this place early this morning, having marched since daylight. . . . For two days we have passed through a splendid country. Great plantations with magnificent residences fill this rich valley of Tuscumbia.

No one who sees the splendor and luxury of these wealthy planters' homes can fail to see that the "Peculiar Institution" has great charms for the rich, and yet no one can fail to see that it is the poor man's bone. We pass these fine plantations and see the slaves toiling for masters and masters' sons who are in the rebel army fighting us, and we let them stay at their toil. A regiment preceeded us a few days ago, and as it passed a cotton-field the whole drove of slaves came to the road and shouted for joy saying, "now we are free!!" One who acted as a forman for the rest said, "take us with you, we will work, we will do anything for you." The Union colonel answered with terrible blasphemy which I will not repeat: "Go back to your plough you black villain or I will put a bullet through you." The poor slaves went back to suffer not only their terrible bitter disappointment but all that is in store for them in consequence of this expression of their wishes. I could chill your blood with the recital of horrors that have resulted to slaves from their expectation of deliverance and their being abandoned to death at the hands of their overseers. But I have not time nor heart to write these things. . . .

Ever your
James

The Virginia Creeper

From the beginning the Union army was plagued by poor leadership. After the North's disastrous defeat at the First Battle of Bull Run, President Lincoln put General George B. McClellan in command of the Army of the Potomac. Through months of hard training, McClellan turned a collection of clumsy, disheartened amateurs into a fine army. But the general had a fatal flaw: excessive caution.

"Nothing but drill and guard duty," wrote Elisha Hunt Rhodes of the Second Rhode Island Infantry. "Even the late battle [Bull Run] has become an old story." Having built a magnificent army, General McClellan was reluctant to risk it in battle. He constantly overestimated the size of the Confederates' forces and called Lincoln "a well-meaning baboon" for urging action. Through the summer and fall of 1861, the general drilled and paraded his troops in Washington. In October he took them into winter quarters.

Finally, in January 1862, Lincoln ran out of patience and ordered McClellan to march on the Confederate capital. The Yankees moved out in mid-March. For the next five months, they campaigned across the Virginia Peninsula, a spit of land between the York and James Rivers leading to Richmond. Again and again McClellan's overcautiousness delayed their progress. At one point the general wasted a month building elaborate fortifications for an assault on Yorktown, which was defended by a force one-tenth his army's size. The night before the planned attack, the Confederates slipped away. McClellan declared a brilliant victory. One of his officers privately nicknamed him the Virginia Creeper.

In June Robert E. Lee took over the defense of Richmond. The Confederate general launched a series of attacks against the Yankees. McClellan's men won nearly every one of these hard-fought battles, but instead of following up on the victories, the Union commander slowly backed down the Peninsula. "This morning we found the entire Army retreating," wrote Elisha Hunt Rhodes in early September. "We took a steamer . . . and went up the Potomac past Washington. . . . It is hard to have reached the point we started from last March, and Richmond is still the Rebel Capital."

Dark Road to Victory

While General McClellan crept across Virginia, President Lincoln was casting about for an able, aggressive leader to take his place. After the bloody Battle of Antietam in September 1862, he fired McClellan and put General Ambrose Burnside in command. Burnside was inexperienced and indecisive. In December 1862 he sacrificed 12,700 men in a suicidal assault on heavily fortified Confederate positions at the Battle of Fredericksburg, Virginia.

Lincoln replaced Burnside with General Joseph Hooker. Promising the "certain destruction" of Lee's army, Hooker devised a "perfect" scheme for ambushing the Confederates at Chancellorsville, Virginia. His plan proved better on paper than in practice: the Battle of Chancellorsville in May 1863 ended in an overwhelming Confederate victory.

By now, morale in the Union army had sunk to an all-time low. The men had suffered through battlefield disasters, disease, exhaustion, and hunger. Although Northern soldiers were generally better fed than the Confederates, their diet consisted mainly of hardtack (hard flour-and-water biscuits), salt pork or beef, and cof-

Union soldiers dig into a rough meal in camp. "Our grub is enough to make a mule desert,"
wrote one Illinois corporal, "and a hog wish he had never been born."

fee. There were times when even these were in short supply. "Food is scarce," wrote
Elisha Hunt Rhodes in 1862. "No bread or salt in the Regiment and I am most
starved. But it is all for the Union and we do not complain."

Not all soldiers were that patient. By February 1863, one-quarter of the Union
army was absent without leave. In March Congress passed the Enrollment Act,
making every male citizen between the ages of twenty and forty-five liable for three
years of military service. Like the Confederate draft, this law favored the rich,
allowing men to escape service by hiring a substitute or paying a three-hundred-
dollar fee. One angry Yankee protested, "A *poor* man's life is as dear as a rich man's."
Another summed up his sagging spirits in a letter to his sister:

> I have nothing cheerfull to write. . . . That delusive fantom of
> hope that has so long burnt dim has at last vanished. . . . The
> great cause of liberty has been managed by Knaves and fools. The
> whole show has been corruption, the result disaster, shame and
> disgrace. . . . Evry thing looks dark.

In the summer of 1863, the Confederates' second invasion of the North reenergized the Union forces. To counter the assault, Lincoln replaced General Hooker with short-tempered but dependable Major General George Gordon Meade. On July 1 Meade's Army of the Potomac and Lee's Army of Northern Virginia fought the Battle of Gettysburg. "Today we have news," a Yankee stationed at a fort in Louisiana wrote home a few days later,

> that [Meade] has whipped Lee. I wish you could have been here to see the boys when they got the news. Cheer after cheer for nearly an hour, one hundred guns from the two forts, everyone seemed as happy as they would be to hear of the death of a rich uncle making them his heirs.

The War in the West

From the start of the war, Union forces enjoyed greater success in the western Confederacy than in the East. In February 1862 General Ulysses S. Grant captured Forts Henry and Donelson on the Tennessee and Cumberland Rivers. The victories gave the Union control of Kentucky and western Tennessee.

In April Grant's army was nearly destroyed in a surprise attack on the banks of the Tennessee River, near Pittsburg Landing. Reinforcements arrived just in time, turning the Battle of Shiloh into a dramatic Union victory, but the losses were staggering. "I saw an open field," the general recalled, "over which the Confederates had made repeated charges . . . , so covered with dead that it would have been possible to walk across . . . in any direction, stepping on dead bodies without a foot touching the ground." Many Northerners denounced Grant as a butcher. Lincoln refused to remove him. "I can't spare this man," the president said. "He fights."

Following Shiloh, a Union navy fleet commanded by David Farragut captured the Mississippi River port city of New Orleans. If the Union could gain complete control of the river, it could cut the South in two, denying the eastern half of the Confederacy supplies and fresh troops from the West. The key to that control was Vicksburg, Mississippi, on a high bluff overlooking the river's east bank. In October 1862 Lincoln gave General Grant the job of putting "the key . . . in our pocket."

The War at Sea

The Union navy provided valuable support during Grant's assault on Vicksburg, both in transporting troops and hammering the rebel defenses. Two years earlier, that navy had consisted of little more than forty wooden warships. After the fall of Fort Sumter in 1861, President Lincoln had ordered a blockade of all Southern ports. To get the job done, the navy had to expand quickly. It bought and armed hundreds of ferries, tugboats, fishing boats, and barges and also began building hundreds of new ships.

The Confederates entered the war with no navy at all. Private shipowners helped fill the gap by smuggling goods past the Union fleet in fast, sleek blockade runners. At the same time, inventive Southern shipbuilders went to work on a secret weapon. Covering the sides of the captured Union frigate the *Merrimack* with iron plates, they created a clumsy, slow-moving, nearly invincible warship. When spies leaked news of this iron monster, Union engineers responded by designing the *Monitor.* Made nearly entirely of iron, this revolutionary ship boasted forty-seven brand-new devices, including a revolving iron gun turret.

The two ironclads met for the first time on March 9, 1862, off the coast of Virginia. Their four-hour duel ended in a draw, without either ship seriously damaging the other. The historic battle marked the end of the age of wooden warships and made every navy in the world obsolete.

Both sides went on to build more ironclads, but the South lacked the materials, manufacturing facilities, and labor force to float a fleet large enough to challenge the Union navy. In the end the North's command of the sea gave it a tremendous advantage that would help sink the Confederate cause.

LIFE ABOARD A UNION WARSHIP COULD BE MONOTONOUS AND UNCOMFORTABLE, AS GEORGE S. GEER OF TROY, NEW YORK, DESCRIBED IN THIS LETTER TO HIS WIFE, MARTHA. GEORGE SERVED AS AN ASSISTANT ENGINEER ABOARD THE *MONITOR*. IN DECEMBER 1862 HE WAS ONE OF THE LAST SAILORS RESCUED WHEN THE SHIP SANK IN A STORM OFF THE COAST OF NORTH CAROLINA.

May 20, 1862

Dear Wife

. . . I told you I would write you how we Live, and what we eat, so I will give you a little sketch in this. To commence, on Sunday as every other day, the Boatswains shrill Whistle is herd [at] six, and every body must turn out and lash their Hammock up and stow them away. All hand[s] make their way on deck, get a pail when their turn comes, and have a good wash. . . . At seven Oclock—as we on ship call it, Six Bells—the Boatswains Whistle is sounded for Grog and Breakfast, which consist of a Pot of Coffee and hard crackers. . . .

After Breakfast, every thing is cleaned up about the Ship, which takes about one hour, and after that there is nothing to do but keep watch. . . .

At twelve the whistle sounds again and Grog and Dinner is the order. . . . For Dinner on Sunday we have Rost Beef put up in cans and preserved Potatoes. The Potatoes taste like I don't know what—any thing that has no taste at all—and the Beef is all parts of the Cow cooked to gather untill it is next to a Jelly and will drop to Pieces. . . .

After dinner it is the same thing—do nothing and sleeping untill five, when Supper is Piped. . . . Our Supper consists of Tea and Crackers. . . . On Mondays, Wednesdays, and Saturdays we have Been Soupe, or perhaps a bettor name would be to call it Bean Water. I am often tempted to strip off my shirt and make a dive and see if there really is Beens in the Bottom that gives it the flavor. I think there must be, but I seldom see them. . . .

Your Affectionate husband,
Geo. S. Geer

Grant tried one scheme after another to move his army east of Vicksburg, the only position from which a successful assault could be launched. Each time he was thwarted by thick woods and swampland, rebel forces, and the city's powerful guns. In the spring of 1863, the general decided on a simple but daring plan. Marching down the west bank of the Mississippi, he ferried his 45,000 troops across the river on Union gunboats. Then the soldiers began the long trek back up through heavily defended Confederate territory. In three weeks they marched 180 miles, living off the land, fighting and winning five battles. On May 14 they captured Jackson, Mississippi. Five days later, they closed in on Vicksburg.

The Siege of Vicksburg

The Union forces suffered severe losses in two direct assaults on the rebel defenses at Vicksburg. Finally, General Grant resolved to take the city by siege. His men dug trenches in lines arcing five miles long in front of Vicksburg. From behind those lines cannons hurled an endless shower of shells, while gunboats pounded the city from the river. "Every day," wrote a Union private, "the regiments, foot by foot, yard by yard, approached nearer the . . . rebel works. We got so we bored like gophers and beavers, with a spade in one hand and a gun in the other."

As their lines crept forward, the men found various ways to relieve their tension and boredom. A "favorite amusement," wrote a Union officer, "was to place a cap on the end of a ramrod and raise it just above the head-logs, betting on the number of bullets which would pass through it within a given time." Captain William T. House of Missouri reported that the Yankees would

> often talk backward and forwards with the Rebels who occupy
> [points] just a little in from ours. . . . Sometimes one of the boys
> will holler . . . , take care of your D——d old head or I'll shoot
> it or get out of the way for I'm going to shoot and after firing
> they'l exclaim how do you like that.

Meanwhile, conditions were becoming increasingly desperate for the 2,500 civilians and 30,000 soldiers trapped inside Vicksburg. Holed up in caves, the towns-

General Ulysses S. Grant (holding a telescope) *directs the siege of Vicksburg, Mississippi, in 1863.*

people lived in constant fear of exploding shells. Their food supplies ran out, and they survived on mule meat, fried rats, and a rubbery bread made of ground corn and peas. Rations for the Confederate troops dropped to one biscuit and a mouthful of bacon per day. On July 4, the fortieth day of the siege, Vicksburg surrendered.

It was a "grand spectacle," wrote William House. "The Rebels Marching out & laying down their arms. . . . Rebeldom is gone out now where we them whiped in this part of the South & the war will end soon & we return to home sweet home."

That prediction was overly optimistic. Nearly two more years of hard fighting lay ahead. But the Confederate losses at Vicksburg, combined with the Union victory at Gettysburg one day earlier, lifted Northern spirits and dealt the South a double blow that in time would prove fatal.

Three

Black Troops Fight for Freedom

Once let the black man get upon his person the brass letters,
U.S., let him get an eagle on his button, and a musket on his
shoulder and bullets in his pockets, and there is no power
on earth which can deny that he has earned the right to
citizenship in the United States.

—FREDERICK DOUGLASS, AUGUST 1863

A War for the Union

In May 1861 three slaves escaped from a Confederate labor battalion to a Union camp at Fortress Monroe, Virginia. According to U.S. government policy, they should have been returned to their master. The North was fighting to preserve the Union, *not* to abolish slavery. But the camp's commander, General Benjamin Butler, refused to send the men back. Instead, he put them to work, labeling them "contraband of war"—property seized for its military value to the enemy.

Congress approved Butler's actions. The First Confiscation Act, passed in August 1861, authorized the army to seize all property, including slaves, that might

A young boy poses proudly after his transformation from "contraband" to Union drummer boy.

be used "in aid of the rebellion." Soon thousands of hungry, homeless "contrabands" were making their way to army refugee camps. Many went to work for the Union as laborers, teamsters, cooks, maids, seamstresses, scouts, and spies.

WHILE MOST WHITE NORTHERNERS VIEWED THE CIVIL WAR AS A BATTLE TO SAVE THE UNION, AFRICAN AMERICANS HAD A DIFFERENT GOAL: FREEDOM. FOR JOHN BOSTON, A RUNAWAY SLAVE FROM MARYLAND WHO FOUND WORK WITH A NEW YORK REGIMENT IN VIRGINIA, THE JOYS OF REACHING SAFETY WERE SHADOWED BY LONGING FOR HIS WIFE, ELIZABETH, WHO REMAINED BEHIND. IT IS NOT KNOWN WHETHER ELIZABETH BOSTON WAS A FREE WOMAN OR A SLAVE, OR WHETHER THE TWO WERE EVER REUNITED.

Upton Hill   January the 12 1862

My Dear Wife   it is with grate joy I take this time to let you know Whare I am   i am now in Safety in the 14th Regiment of Brooklyn   this Day I can Adress you thank god as a free man   I had a little truble in giting away   But as the lord led the Children of Isrel to the land of Canon [Canaan] So he led me to a land Whare fredom Will rain in spite Of earth and hell   Dear you must make your Self content   i am free from al the Slavers Lash and as you have chose the Wise plan Of Serving the lord i hope you Will pray Much and i Will try by the help of god To Serv him With all my hart   I am With a very nice man and have All that hart Can Wish But My Dear I Cant express my grate desire that i Have to See you   i trust the time Will Come When We Shal meet again And if We dont met on earth We Will Meet in heven Whare Jesas ranes   Dear Elizabeth tell Mrs Ownees [Owens] That i trust that She Will Continue Her kindness to you and that god Will Bless her on earth and Save her In grate eternity   My Acomplements To Mrs Owens and her Children   may They Prosper through life   I never Shall forgit her kindness to me Dear Wife i must Close   rest yourself Contented i am free i Want you to rite To me Soon as you Can Without Delay . . .

> *Your Affectionate Husban . . .*
> *John Boston*

Legally, contrabands were not free. By early 1862, however, the North was inching toward emancipation. Frustrated and angered by battlefield losses, Northerners were eager to punish Southern slaveholders. They also had begun to realize how valuable the slaves who labored in Southern farm fields and army camps were to the enemy's war effort—and how useful they could be to the Union cause. According to one Illinois infantryman, every Union regiment stationed in the South had contrabands working as "teamsters and cooks, which puts that many more men back in the ranks. . . . It will make a difference in the regt [regiment] of not less than 75 men that will carry guns that did not before."

Fugitive slaves cross a river in Virginia, on their journey to safety and freedom behind Union lines.

In September 1862, five days after the Union victory at Antietam, President Lincoln issued the preliminary Emancipation Proclamation. When it took effect on January 1, 1863, the proclamation freed all slaves in areas in rebellion against the Union. White Northerners were divided in their reactions. Some critics opposed emancipation, while others denounced the president for leaving slavery untouched in the loyal border states. Practical-minded supporters saw the act as a means of weakening the Confederacy and ending the war. Devoted abolitionists praised Lincoln for elevating the conflict from a mere struggle between North and South to "a contest between human rights and human liberty on one side and eternal bondage on the other."

Among African Americans the verdict was unanimous: The Emancipation Proclamation was a beacon of joy and promise. It gave word that the North was no longer fighting for the old Union but for a new nation where all would be free.

A Chance to Fight

The Emancipation Proclamation approved the recruitment of African-American men into the Union army. Since the beginning of the conflict, blacks who had pressed for the opportunity to serve had been told, "This is a white man's war." Most white Northerners believed that former slaves were too timid to fight, and they objected to serving side by side with blacks. As one New York infantryman put it, "We think we are a too superior race for that."

Those attitudes changed as soldiers began to realize that enlisting blacks could save white lives. After all, a black man in uniform could stop a rebel bullet just as well as a white man. Expanding the army with black regiments also might hasten the war's end. "[It is] no disgrace to me to have black men for soldiers," wrote Sergeant Edwin Payne of Illinois. "If they can kill rebels I say arm them and set them to shooting."

The first regiment of freed slaves was sworn into the Union army in South Carolina in November 1862. By the summer of 1863, some thirty black regiments bore arms and dozens more were being formed. Black recruits faced the same difficulties as whites. They endured the same bad food and cold winter quarters, the dirt and disease, the hard hours of drilling, boredom, and loneliness. But African Americans carried an added burden: racial discrimination.

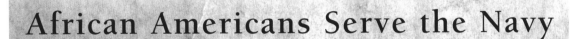

African Americans Serve the Navy

While African Americans pushed for the right to join the Union army, thousands were already serving at sea. Since 1813 the U.S. Navy had enlisted free "persons of color." Black and white sailors usually served side by side. A few ships were manned entirely by black sailors commanded by white officers.

The navy also received valuable services from black civilians. One of the most famous was Robert Smalls. As a slave in Charleston, South Carolina, Robert worked on the Confederate ship the *Planter*, based in Charleston Harbor. On May 12, 1862, he was left to watch over a valuable cargo of military supplies while the ship's officers went ashore for the night. Robert slipped his brother, a few friends, and their wives and children aboard. The next morning he eased the *Planter* from the dock and past the Confederate guns at Fort Sumter, saluting with the ship's signal whistle to avoid suspicion. As the Confederate vessel neared a U.S. Navy ship, Robert raised a white flag, "stepped forward, and taking off his hat, shouted, 'Good morning, sir! I've brought you some of the old United States guns, sir!' "

For his daring deed Robert Smalls and his crew were awarded half the prize money for the *Planter*. Robert went on to pilot several Union blockade vessels, and after the war he became one of the South's most influential black political leaders.

Slave-turned-Union-hero Robert Smalls

"Instead of the musket It is the spad[e] and the Whelbarrow and the Axe," complained one black soldier. African Americans were assigned more than their share of menial tasks: hauling logs, building earthworks, digging trenches. They were segregated in all-black regiments, nearly always commanded by white officers. Most intolerable of all, black soldiers were paid less than whites. While white privates earned thirteen dollars a month plus clothing, blacks were paid ten dollars *minus* a three-dollar clothing allowance.

Rather than submit to this injustice, several black regiments refused to accept any wages at all. The Fifty-fourth Massachusetts Volunteer Infantry, the first regiment of free blacks organized in the North, served for eighteen months without pay. "We are men and will do our duty," wrote Corporal James Henry Gooding in August 1863, "as we have done always, before and since that day we were offered to sell our manhood for ten dollars per month." The men would not receive any wages until late 1864, after Congress finally passed a law granting black soldiers equal pay.

The Test of Battle

Even as they struggled against discrimination and injustice, black troops were earning a reputation for courage under fire. In May 1863 two black regiments from Louisiana fought heroically in an attack on Port Hudson, a Confederate stronghold on the lower Mississippi River. In June two regiments of former slaves beat back a Confederate assault on Milliken's Bend, a Union outpost in Louisiana. Then, on July 18, the Fifty-fourth Massachusetts was chosen to lead an assault on Fort Wagner, at the entrance to Charleston Harbor.

A narrow stretch of beach led to the fort. Charging across the sand, the six hundred men of the Fifty-fourth encountered a blinding sheet of musket and artillery fire. Those who made it off the beach scrambled through a half-filled moat and up the high wall of the rebel fortifications. "We met the foe on the parapet of Wagner with the bayonet," recalled James Henry Gooding. "We were exposed to a murderous fire from the batteries of the fort, from our Monitors [ships] and our land batteries. . . . Mortal men could not stand such a fire, and the assault on Wagner was a failure."

The Fifty-fourth Massachusetts lost 272 men—nearly half its force—including its young white commander, Colonel Robert Shaw. Although the attack had failed, in a larger sense it was a historic victory. The accounts of the regiment's unflinching courage silenced the critics of black enlistment and emancipation. Weeks later, the New York *Tribune* summed up the battle's significance:

> It is not too much to say that if this Massachusetts Fifty-fourth had faltered when its trial came, two hundred thousand colored troops for whom it was a pioneer would never have been put into the field. . . . But it did not falter. It made Fort Wagner such a name to the colored race as Bunker Hill has been for nearly ninety years to the white Yankees.

The men of the all-black Fifty-fourth Massachusetts Volunteer Infantry charge into the rebel guns at Fort Wagner, July 18, 1863. One survivor wrote to his mother, "They mowed us down like grass."

THE FAMOUS AFRICAN-AMERICAN WRITER, PUBLISHER, AND ABOLITIONIST FREDERICK DOUGLASS CALLED THE CIVIL WAR A "GOLDEN OPPORTUNITY" FOR BLACKS TO STRIKE A BLOW AGAINST SLAVERY AND LAY THE GROUNDWORK FOR FULL EQUALITY. DOUGLASS TRAVELED THROUGHOUT THE NORTH RECRUITING VOLUNTEERS FOR THE FIFTY-FOURTH MASSACHUSETTS VOLUNTEER INFANTRY. AMONG THE FIRST TO JOIN WERE TWO OF HIS SONS, LEWIS AND CHARLES. BOTH MEN SURVIVED THE HEROIC ASSAULT ON FORT WAGNER. TWO DAYS AFTER THE BATTLE, LEWIS DOUGLASS WROTE TO HIS FIANCÉE, AMELIA LOGUEN.

Morris Island. S.C. July 20 [1863]

My Dear Amelia:

I have been in two fights, and am unhurt. I am about to go in another I believe to-night. Our men fought well on both occasions. The last was desperate   we charged that terrible battery on Morris Island known as Fort Wagoner, and were repulsed with a loss of [many] killed and wounded. I escaped unhurt from amidst that perfect hail of shot and shell. It was terrible. I need not particularize   the papers will give a better [report] than I have time to give. My thoughts are with you often, you are as dear as ever, be good enough to remember it as I no doubt you will. As I said before we are on the eve of another fight and I am very busy and have just snatched a moment to write you. . . . Should I fall in the next fight killed or wounded I hope to fall with my face to the foe. . . .

This regiment has established its reputation as a fighting regiment   not a man flinched, though it was a trying time. Men fell all around me. A shell would explode and clear a space of twenty feet, our men would close up again, but it was no use we had to retreat, which was a very hazardous undertaking. How I got out of that fight alive I cannot tell, but I am here. My Dear girl I hope again to see you. I must bid you farewell should I be killed. Remember if I die I die in a good cause. I wish we had a hundred thousand colored troops   we would put an end to this war. Good Bye to all.

Your own loving,

Lewis

"Blood of the Slaughtered"

From their first action it became clear that black troops faced even greater perils than whites on the field of battle. As one man from North Carolina observed, the Confederates "were perfectly exasperated at the idea of negroes opposed to them & rushed at them like so many devils." Blacks who were captured were treated not as prisoners of war but rather as criminals guilty of rebelling against their white masters.

Following the battles of Port Hudson and Milliken's Bend, reports reached the North that the Confederates had hanged a number of black prisoners. In July 1863 President Lincoln threatened to retaliate, executing one rebel soldier "for every soldier of the United States killed in violation of the laws of war." Later, he halted all exchanges of Union and Confederate prisoners because the South refused to include black soldiers and their officers.

Despite these actions the atrocities continued. Some captured black soldiers were turned over to local Southern authorities and executed; others were sold into slavery. In at least one instance, after the Confederates captured Fort Pillow, Tennessee, in April 1864, rebel soldiers massacred hundreds of unarmed black troops as they tried to surrender. "The river was dyed with the blood of the slaughtered for two hundred yards," reported Confederate commander Nathan Bedford Forrest. "It is hoped that these facts will demonstrate to the Northern people that Negro soldiers cannot cope with Southerners."

Such actions did not stop African Americans from fighting with spirit and determination. In fact, the knowledge that they "fought with ropes round their necks" inspired black troops to even greater ferocity. According to one white soldier from Pennsylvania, the rebels were "not as much afraid of us as they are of the [black troops]. When they charge they will not take any prisoners, if they can help it. Their cry is, 'Remember Fort Pillow!' "

By the war's end, about 180,000 African Americans had worn the Union uniform—nearly 10 percent of the Northern army. Their service gave pride and confidence to a long-oppressed people and strengthened the former slaves' claim to freedom. In the postwar years the memory of black contributions to Union victory would inspire all African Americans in their struggle for full equality.

MILITARY SERVICE GAVE MANY FORMER SLAVES THEIR FIRST TASTE OF SELF-CONFIDENCE AND POWER. SPOTSWOOD RICE, A SLAVE-TURNED-SOLDIER FROM MISSOURI, GAINED THE COURAGE TO CHALLENGE HIS FORMER OWNER, KITTEY DIGGS, WHO STILL HELD HIS DAUGHTER, MARY. RICE SWORE TO RETURN WITH THE POWER AND AUTHORITY OF THE UNION ARMY BEHIND HIM AND RESCUE MARY FROM SLAVERY.

[September 3, 1864]

I received a letter . . . telling me that you say I tried to steal to plunder my Child away from you now I want you to understand that Mary is my Child and she is a God given rite of my own and you may hold on to hear as long as you can but I want you to remember this one thing that the longer you keep my Child from me the longer you will have to burn in hell and the quicer youll get their for we are now makeing up about one thoughsand blacke troops to come up . . . and when we come woe be to . . . the Slaveholding rebbels for we dont expect to leave them there root neor branch . . . I want you to understand kittey diggs that where ever you and I meets we are enmays [enemies] to each other I offered once to pay you forty dollars for my own Child but I am glad now that you did not accept it Just hold on now as long as you can and the worse it will be for you you never in your life befor I came down hear did you give [my] Children any thing not eny thing whatever not even a dollers worth of expencs now you call my children your pro[per]ty not so with me my Children is my own and I expect to get them and when I get ready to come after Mary I will have bout a powrer and autherity to bring hear away and to exacute vengencens [vengeance] on them that holds my Child

* you will then know how to talke to me I will assure that and you will know how to talk rite too I want you now to just hold on to hear if you want to if your conchosense [conscience] tells thats the road go that road and what it will brig you to kittey diggs I have no fears about geting Mary out of your hands this whole Government gives chear to me and you cannot help your self*

Four

Women at the Front

I saw, crowded into one old sunken hotel, lying upon its bare, wet, bloody floors, 500 fainting men hold up their cold, bloodless, dingy hands as I passed, and beg me in Heaven's name for a cracker to keep them from starving.

—UNION NURSE CLARA BARTON

Civil War Heroines

In the mid-1800s the United States was half a century away from the day when women would be welcomed into the armed forces. Nevertheless, women made valuable contributions during the Civil War years. Most of their work was done on the homefront. When men went to war, the women they left behind managed the farms and businesses, worked in offices and factories, and struggled to hold home and family together in the face of severe shortages, losses, and danger.*

*For more on women's homefront contributions, see this book's companion volume, LETTERS FROM THE HOMEFRONT: THE CIVIL WAR.

A smaller but still significant number of women were not content to remain at home. These Civil War heroines served on the front lines, working as army nurses, scouts, spies, and soldiers in disguise.

Angels of the Battlefield

"Almost every house in the city was a private hospital, and almost every woman a nurse," recalled a Richmond woman. When Confederate and Yankee armies clashed, any front yard could become a battlefield. Women sometimes found themselves taking the wounded into their homes or tending fallen soldiers in the streets. Thousands of women volunteered to travel with the armies as nurses. They worked in field hospitals set up close to the battlefront and on transport ships or trains carrying wounded men to behind-the-lines hospitals.

Wounded Union soldiers are carried by ambulance wagon from the battlefield to a field hospital.

"Nothing that I had ever heard or read had given me the faintest idea of the horrors witnessed here," Kate Cumming confided to her diary in April 1862. A patriotic young Alabama woman, Cumming had volunteered to work at a Confederate hospital set up in a Mississippi hotel to treat casualties from the Battle of Shiloh. She found men

> lying all over the house, on their blankets, just as they were brought from the battle-field. They are in the hall, on the gallery, and crowded into very small rooms. The foul air from this mass of human beings at first made me giddy and sick, but I soon got over it.

Like most of the war nurses, Cumming had no medical training. In fact, she had "never seen a wounded man." But within a few days, she was cleaning and bandaging wounds, feeding men and reading to them, comforting the sick and the dying.

AMONG THE MANY BRAVE WOMEN WHO VOLUNTEERED AS CIVIL WAR NURSES WAS THIRTY-YEAR-OLD LOUISA MAY ALCOTT OF CONCORD, MASSACHUSETTS. IN DECEMBER 1862 LOUISA WENT TO WORK AT A UNION ARMY HOSPITAL IN WASHINGTON, D.C., "DETERMINED TO MAKE THE SOLDIERS JOLLY." THE LETTERS SHE WROTE HOME WERE COLLECTED AND PUBLISHED IN 1863 AS *HOSPITAL SKETCHES*. IN THIS EXCERPT FROM THAT BOOK, LOUISA DESCRIBES HER INTRODUCTION TO THE TASK OF BATHING AND FEEDING THE WOUNDED. A FEW YEARS AFTER THE WAR'S END, LOUISA MAY ALCOTT EARNED FAME AS THE AUTHOR OF *LITTLE WOMEN* AND OTHER NOVELS.

"They've come! they've come! hurry up, ladies—you're wanted."

"Who have come? the rebels?"

This sudden summons in the gray dawn was somewhat startling to a three days' nurse like myself, and, as the thundering knock came at our door, I sprang up in my bed.
. . .

"Bless you, no child; it's the wounded from Fredericksburg; forty ambulances are at the door, and we shall have our hands full in fifteen minutes." . . .

The sight of several stretchers, each with its legless, armless, or desperately wound-ed occupant, entering my ward, admonished me that I was there to work, not to wonder or weep; so I corked up my feelings, and returned to the path of duty. . . .

"Come, my dear, begin to wash as fast as you can. Tell them to take off socks, coats and shirts, scrub them well, put on clean shirts, and the attendants will finish them off, and lay them in bed."

If she had requested me to shave them all, or dance a hornpipe on the stove funnel, I should have been less staggered; but to scrub some dozen lords of creation at a moment's notice, was really—really—. However, there was no time for nonsense, and, having resolved when I came to do everything I was bid, I drowned my scruples [mis-givings] in my wash-bowl, clutched my soap manfully, and, assuming a business-like air, made a dab at the first dirty specimen I saw. . . . I chanced to light on a withered old Irishman, wounded in the head, which caused that portion of his frame to be tastefully laid out like a garden, the bandages being the walks, his hair the shrubbery. He was so overpowered by the honor of having a lady wash him, as he expressed it, that he did nothing but roll up his eyes, and bless me, in an irresistible style which was too much for my sense of the ludicrous; so we laughed together, and when I knelt down to take off his shoes, he "flopped" also, and wouldn't hear of my touching "them dirty craters. May your bed above be aisy darlin', for the day's work ye are doon!—Woosh! there ye are, and bedad, it's hard tellin' which is the dirtiest, the fut or the shoe." . . .

Having done up our human wash, and laid it out to dry, the second syllable of our version of the word war-fare was enacted with much success. Great trays of bread, meat, soup and coffee appeared; and both nurses and attendants turned waiters, serving boun-tiful rations to all who could eat. . . . Very welcome seemed the generous meal, after a week of suffering, exposure, and short commons; soon the brown faces began to smile, as food, warmth, and rest, did their pleasant work; and the grateful "Thank'ees" were followed by more graphic accounts of the battle and retreat, than any paid reporter could have given us.

It was exhausting work. Nurses labored long hours in overcrowded facilities, sur-rounded by deadly diseases and horrible wounds. Medical care was primitive in Civil War times. Doctors knew very little about the causes of disease and infection or the need

Clara Barton worked tirelessly as a nurse in Union army camps and on the battlefields. After the war she founded the American Red Cross.

for sanitation. Wounded arms and legs were amputated by "sawbones" wearing blood-stained aprons and wielding dirty knives and sponges. Infection and then gangrene often set in, followed by a slow, agonizing death. "Tis hard to see them die one after another & not be able to help them in any way," wrote Confederate nurse Ada Bacot.

Added to these trials were the dangers of flying lead. The famous Union nurse Clara Barton, known as the Angel of the Battlefield, sometimes worked with her face blue from gunpowder "while the shells were bursting in every direction." At the Battle of Antietam, Barton was so close to the action that she had to take over for a surgeon who was killed while drinking from a cup she had handed him.

With all its demands, nursing was a positive experience for most women. Working outside the home and proving their competence under challenging conditions gave them self-confidence and satisfaction. "I have never worked so hard in all my life," wrote one Southern nurse, "and I would rather do [this] than anything else in the world."

Spies for the Cause

Some of the Civil War's best secret agents were women. Not only were women less likely than men to be suspected of spying, but they also were generally punished less severely if they were caught.

One of the most famous Confederate spies was Rose O'Neal Greenhow. A leading lady of Washington society, Greenhow used her "almost irresistible seductive powers" to charm secrets out of Union military and political leaders. Her most important mission turned the course of the First Battle of Bull Run. Learning that Northern troops were on the march, Greenhow sent a coded message, rolled up in a friend's long hair, to Confederate General Pierre Beauregard. Her information helped the general prepare his forces and defeat the Yankees. After the battle Greenhow was arrested. "I had no reason to fear," she wrote in her memoirs. "I had

Southern spy Rose O'Neal Greenhow, with her daughter, at Washington's Old Capitol Prison

a right to my own political opinions. I am a Southern woman, born with Revolutionary blood in my veins. Freedom of speech and of thought were my birthright, guaranteed, signed and sealed by the blood of our fathers."

ONE OF THE MOST SENSATIONAL SOUTHERN SPIES WAS BELLE BOYD, KNOWN AS LA BELLE REBELLE. JUST SEVENTEEN YEARS OLD WHEN THE WAR BEGAN, BOYD BECAME A CONFEDERATE COURIER, CARRYING MESSAGES THROUGH THE UNION LINES. SHE WAS ARRESTED SIX TIMES FOR SPYING. IN HER AUTOBIOGRAPHY, *BELLE BOYD: IN CAMP AND PRISON,* SHE EXPLAINED HOW SHE CONTINUED HER CLOAK-AND-DAGGER ACTIVITIES WHILE CONFINED IN WASHINGTON'S CARROLL PRISON IN THE SUMMER OF 1863.

One evening, about nine o'clock, while seated at my window, I was . . . startled . . . by hearing something whiz by my head into the room and strike the wall beyond. . . . I saw, to my astonishment, that it was an arrow which had struck the wall opposite my window; and fastened to this arrow was a letter; I immediately tore it open, and found that it contained the following words:—

"Poor girl, you have the deepest sympathy of all the best community in Washington City. . . . If you will listen attentively to the instructions that I give you, you will be able to correspond with and hear from your friends outside.

"On Thursdays and Saturdays, in the evening, just after twilight, I will come into the square opposite the prison. . . . I will then shoot an arrow into your room, as I have done this evening, with a letter attached. Do not be alarmed, as I am a good shot.

"The manner in which you will reply to these messages will be in this way: Procure a large india-rubber ball; open it, and place your communication within it, written on foreign paper; then sew it together. . . . Then throw the ball, with as much force as you can exert, across the street into the square, and trust to me, I will get it. . . ."

It was an easy thing for me to procure an india-rubber ball without subjecting myself to the least suspicion; and by this means I commenced a correspondence which I had no reason to regret; for whoever the mysterious personage may have been, he was, without doubt, honorable and sincere in his profession of sympathy.

Through him I became possessed of much valuable information regarding the movement of the Federals . . .

Harriet Tubman, one of the most successful "conductors" on the Underground Railroad, served the Union army as nurse, scout, and spy.

Equally resolute were the women who spied for the Union. These included a number of African-American women, both enslaved and free. One of the best known was Harriet Tubman. An escaped slave, Tubman had returned south many times to help more than three hundred enslaved men, women, and children reach freedom through the Underground Railroad. During the war, she worked as a nurse, cook, scout, and spy for Union troops in South Carolina. Disguising herself as an old slave woman, the forty-year-old Tubman moved easily through rebel territory, gathering intelligence on the location of Southern stockpiles of ammunition, cotton, food, and other supplies.

In July 1863 Tubman led Union troops on an expedition in South Carolina's Combahee River territory. The soldiers destroyed millions of dollars' worth of enemy property and freed more than 750 slaves. "This is the only military command in America," reported a Union officer, "wherein a woman, black or white, led the raid and under whose inspiration it was originated and conducted."

The Boys' War

Some women disguised themselves as men and served as soldiers in the Union and Confederate armies. One of the reasons they were able to blend in was the presence of so many young, slightly built, beardless boys. While the minimum age for enlistment was eighteen, boys as young as nine could sign on as drummer boys and buglers. Also, many teenage boys lied about their age to join the army, especially during the early wave of war enthusiasm. Estimates put the number of under-eighteen soldiers on both sides at anywhere from 250,000 to 420,000.

Several boy soldiers were cited for bravery. During a battle outside Atlanta in 1864, Eddie Evans of Mississippi, "a mere boy, . . . took his stand in advance of the line without any protection in an open field, . . . waving his colors defiantly and called upon his comrades to rally to the flag." At the Battle of Shiloh, Private David Camp, "only fourteen years old, served as No. 5 man at the left [artillery] piece with the skill and bravery of an old soldier."

The Battle of Chickamauga in September 1863 made eleven-year-old Union drummer boy Johnny Clem a legend. When a Confederate colonel tried to capture the artillery wagon on which Johnny was riding, the boy shot and killed the officer with a short-ened rifle that had been specially made for him by the men of his regiment. After the war the "Drummer Boy of Chickamauga" remained in the army, retiring as a major general shortly before World War I.

A Confederate "boy soldier," around 1863

Soldiers in Disguise

No one knows for certain how many of the Civil War's three million soldiers were women. Although women were not permitted to enlist on either side, an estimated four hundred or more cut their hair, put on men's clothing, and marched off to war. Some craved adventure and independence. Some simply wanted to stay with their soldier husbands. Others felt an irresistible call to "do something for our Country."

How did women soldiers escape detection? Physical examinations for Civil War recruits often included little more than a quick check to make sure the prospect could march and use his trigger finger. Soldiers wore loose-fitting uniforms. Because they bathed and relieved themselves outdoors, privacy was possible. In fact, many women probably were never discovered and some went undetected for months or years, until they were killed or required emergency medical treatment. "We discovered last week a soldier who turned out to be a girl," wrote an Indiana cavalryman in 1863. "She had already been in service for 21 months and was twice wounded. Maybe she would have remained undiscovered for a long time if she hadn't fainted. She was given a warm bath which gave the secret away."

Some women took their deception a step further, combining soldiering with spying. Twenty-year-old Sarah Emma Edmonds enlisted in a Michigan regiment in 1861 as Frank Thompson. She served for two years as a hospital orderly, mail carrier, and colonel's aide, and took part in several battles, including First Bull Run and Antietam. The intrepid private also went on intelligence-gathering missions behind Confederate lines, sometimes "disguised" as a woman.

Early in 1863 Emma became ill with malaria and was forced to leave camp to seek treatment in a private hospital. Frank Thompson was labeled a deserter, and Emma Edmonds stepped back into her skirts to work as a nurse for the rest of the war. "I am naturally fond of adventure," she later wrote, "a little ambitious, and a good deal romantic—but patriotism was the true secret of my success."

LYONS WAKEMAN OF THE 153RD NEW YORK STATE VOLUNTEERS WAS NOT QUITE WHAT HE SEEMED. IN REALITY, THE FIVE-FOOT-TALL PRIVATE WAS SARAH ROSETTA WAKEMAN, A NEW YORK FARM GIRL. ROSETTA DISGUISED HERSELF AS A MAN AND ENLISTED IN THE ARMY IN AUGUST 1862 TO SEEK ADVENTURE AND EARN MONEY TO HELP PAY HER FAMILY'S DEBTS. SHE SERVED IN THE DEFENSE OF WASHINGTON AND IN A HARD CAMPAIGN IN LOUISIANA, MARCHING SEVEN HUNDRED MILES ON BAD FOOD AND FOUL WATER. LIKE MANY OF HER FELLOW SOLDIERS, ROSETTA DEVELOPED DYSENTERY (SEVERE DIARRHEA). SHE DIED ON JUNE 19, 1864, BUT HER TRUE IDENTITY REMAINED A SECRET FOR MORE THAN A CENTURY, UNTIL HER LETTERS FROM THE BATTLEFRONT WERE PUBLISHED IN THE 1990S.

Alexandria, Virginia
June the 5, 1863

Dear Parents,
It is with Affectionate love that I Write to you and let you know that I am well at Present and enjoying myself the best I can. . . .

I can tell you what made me leave home. It was because I had got tired of stay[ing] in that neighborhood. I knew that I Could help you more to leave home than to stay there with you. So I left. I am not sorry that I left you. I believe that it will be all for the best yet. I believe that God will spare my life to come home once more. When I get out of this war I will come home and see you but I Shall not stay long before I shall be off to take care of my Self. I will help you all I can as long as I live. . . .

I [am] enjoying my Self better this summer than I ever did before in this world. I have good Clothing and enough to eat and nothing to do, only to handle my gun and that I can do as well as the rest of them.

I don't want you to mourn about me for I can take care of my Self and I know my business as well as other folks know them for me. I will Dress as I am a mind to for all anyone else [cares], and if they don't let me Alone they will be sorry for it. . . .

I can't think of anything more to Write, so good-by for this time.

Rosetta Wakeman

Five

"Desolation and Ashes"

If anyone had told me before the war that men could have borne for month

after month . . . what we have, I would have thought it all talk.

I recollect when we first came into the service we grumbled at fare

that we would now think the greatest luxuries.

—ALABAMA CAPTAIN BOLLING HALL, APRIL 15, 1864

Total War

After its losses at Gettysburg and Vicksburg in July 1863, the Confederacy was broken in two. Still, Southerners clung to hope. If they could just hold out long enough, perhaps the North would tire of the terrible costs of war and let the South go.

For their part, Union military leaders only became more committed to total war as the conflict dragged on. The time for targeting the Confederate army alone was past. The only way to force the South to surrender, argued General Ulysses S. Grant, was to defeat not only its military forces but also the fighting spirit of its people. "I gave up all idea," the general wrote, "of saving the Union except by complete conquest."

Ulysses S. Grant, general in chief of the Union army and, later, America's eighteenth president

IN SEPTEMBER 1863, 60,000 YANKEES FACED AN EQUAL NUMBER OF CONFEDERATES A FEW MILES BELOW CHATTANOOGA, TENNESSEE, BESIDE A CREEK CALLED CHICKAMAUGA, FROM AN OLD CHEROKEE WORD MEANING "RIVER OF DEATH." THE ARMIES FOUGHT A FURIOUS TWO-DAY BATTLE THAT CLAIMED NEARLY 35,000 CASUALTIES AND SENT THE UNION TROOPS FLEEING BACK NORTH. FOLLOWING THE BATTLE OF CHICKAMAUGA, JOSHUA CALLAWAY OF THE 28TH ALABAMA INFANTRY SENT HIS WIFE, DULCINEA, A LONG LETTER THAT INCLUDED THIS ACCOUNT OF THE SECOND DAY OF FIGHTING, ON SEPTEMBER 20. JOSHUA WAS KILLED TWO MONTHS LATER DURING A UNION ASSAULT ON CHATTANOOGA.

Camp of wagon train 28th Ala Vols.
Sunday September 24th 1863

Mrs. Dulcinea B. Callaway:
. . . At 8 o'clock Sunday morning, the 20th, the battle commenced, away down on the right several miles, with increased fury, and kept coming up along the line till at 10 the whole line—which I suppose was some 6 or 8 miles long—became engaged. We, being on the extreme left, were ordered forward.

We threw out a line of skirmishers a hundred and fifty yards in front and moved steadily forward not knowing how far off the enemy was. When we had gone about three hundred yards our skirmishers encountered those of the enemy, and as soon as the firing commenced all order and control was lost, the men raised the "War whoop," "the yell," "The battle cry" and away they went like a gang of mad tigers or demons. . . . We soon ran over our skirmishers and those of the enemy fled as if old Scratch [the devil] had been after them. Thus we charged fully half a mile across an old field then across a skirt of woods then another old field and into another skirt of woods. . . .

Our Brigade was then ordered farther to the right and formed at the foot of a long hill on the top of which was the enemy's line. It was now 2 o'clock in the evening and the battle was raging all along the line on our left and right as if heaven and earth were coming together. A thousand thunderstorms all turned loose together could not equal the noise.

We were now ordered forward and when we got half way up the hill they opened on us with great fury with grape[shot] and canister [artillery shells] and with small arms. But we moved steadily on till we got in about twenty yards of their line where we halted and went regularly to work. Here commenced a scene that beggars description, and God forbid that I should ever have to witness such another. The carnage was awful. Men were shot down all around me. I was indeed in the very midst of death. We fought them thus close I suppose about ten minutes when, as if by command, our whole line gave way and away we went down the hill like a gang of sheep. . . . We fell back about two hundred yards and rallied and then advanced again to within about fifty yards of our former position. . . . We held that ground fifteen or twenty minutes and gave way again, but rallied as before and moved a third time to the charge. This time we reached the crest or top of the hill and found ourselves on equal footing with the enemy. Here we stood at least an hour before they gave way. . . and fled in every direction. . . .

I have now seen and experienced "The horrors of war" as well as the spoils and glories. And may God deliver us from so awful a scourge and calamity! . . .

Your Loving
J. K. Callaway

The Union Advances

A few weeks after the Confederate victory at Chickamauga, General Grant was placed in command of all Western armies. Grant struck back at the rebels, driving them out of Tennessee and into Georgia. With that victory the Union won the war in the West.

Grant was rewarded with a newly created post: general in chief of all U.S. armies. He devised a plan for defeating the Confederacy by striking on several fronts at once. To lead the advance in Georgia, he chose his most trusted commander, General William T. Sherman. Grant instructed Sherman to "get into the interior of the enemy's country as far as you can, inflicting all the damage you can against their war resources."

Sherman's army moved into Georgia in May 1864. For three miserable months the men marched under a blazing sun, along dusty roads and through

General William T. Sherman led the Union advance on Atlanta in 1864. After capturing the city, he promised to "make Georgia howl" with his march across the state, to Savannah.

woods filled with crawling, biting insects. Rebel forces struck again and again, desperately trying to halt their advance. But the Yankees outnumbered the Confederates almost two to one. Step by step they forced the enemy to fall back. By late July, Northern and Southern troops stood face-to-face on the outskirts of Atlanta.

The armies fought three hard battles outside the Georgia capital. Then the rebels withdrew into the city. For the next four weeks, Union guns pounded Atlanta, with a "constant roaring of cannon and rattling of musketry" that sounded to one resident like "tens of thousands of shots blending into one great continuous whole." On September 1 the exhausted Confederates evacuated the city. Sherman sent President Lincoln a triumphant telegram: "Atlanta is ours, and fairly won."

Campaigns of Destruction

As Sherman's army marched into Atlanta, the Confederacy was under fire on other fronts as well. A few weeks earlier, General Philip Sheridan and 45,000 Union troops had swept into the Shenandoah Valley. The Confederate army had long used this broad, fertile region in northern Virginia as both an invasion route and a food basket. Now Grant ordered Sheridan to strip the land so thoroughly that "crows flying over it for the balance of the season will have to carry their provender [food]."

The Yankee troops carried out their orders with grim efficiency. They burned barns, mills, and crops and killed or drove off all the livestock. By the time they finished in mid-October, Sheridan could report that the valley was a wasteland, its people "left nothing but their eyes to weep with."

Farther south, Sherman's army carried the campaign of destruction deep into the heart of the Confederacy. After taking Atlanta, the general had ordered all civilians out of the city. In mid-November he set Atlanta ablaze. Then he started his 62,000 men on a March to the Sea.

WHEN GENERAL SHERMAN ORDERED ALL CIVILIANS TO EVACUATE CAPTURED ATLANTA, CITY OFFICIALS PROTESTED THAT THE ORDER WOULD CAUSE "APPALLING AND HEART-RENDING" HARDSHIPS. IN HIS REPLY SHERMAN RESTATED THE PRINCIPLES THAT HAD LED THE UNION TO WAR AND ARGUED THAT THE ONLY WAY FOR THE SOUTH TO ESCAPE THE UNAVOIDABLE CRUELTIES OF WAR WAS BY ENDING ITS RESISTANCE.

Atlanta, Georgia
September 12, 1864.

James M. Calhoun, Mayor, E. E. Rawson and S. C. Wells, representing city Council of Atlanta.

Gentlemen: I have your letter of the 11th, in the nature of a petition to revoke my orders removing all the inhabitants from Atlanta. I have read it carefully, and give full credit to your statements of the distress that will be occasioned, and yet shall not revoke my orders, because they were not designed to meet the humanities of the case, but to prepare for the future struggles in which millions of good people outside of Atlanta have a deep interest. We must have peace, not only at Atlanta, but in all America. To secure this, we must stop the war that now desolates our once happy and favored country. To stop war, we must defeat the rebel armies which are arrayed against the laws and Constitution that all must respect and obey. . . .

War is cruelty, and you cannot refine it; and those who brought war into our country deserve all the curses . . . a people can pour out. I know I had no hand in making this war, and I know I will make more sacrifices to-day than any of you to secure peace. But you cannot have peace and a division of our country. If the United States submits to a division now, it will not stop, but will go on until we reap the fate of . . . eternal war. . . .

You might as well appeal against the thunder-storm as against these terrible hardships of war. They are inevitable, and the only way the people of Atlanta can hope once more to live in peace and quiet at home, is to stop the war, which can only be done by admitting that it began in error and is perpetuated in pride. . . .

But, my dear sirs, when peace does come, you may call on me for any thing. Then will I share with you the last cracker, and watch with you to shield your homes and families against danger from every quarter. . . .

Yours in haste,
W. T. Sherman, Major-General commanding.

All along their line of march, Sherman's troops looted mansions and farmyards, enjoying an endless feast of fresh ham and chicken, pickles and sweet potatoes, flour, eggs, and butter. "This is probably the greatest pleasure excursion ever planned," wrote a Union soldier. "It already beats everything I ever saw soldiering, and promises to prove much richer yet."

What the men couldn't eat or carry off, they destroyed. Bridges, warehouses, homes, barns, and crops were burned, and railroad ties were pried up and twisted. One Southern woman watched as

> the lurid flames of burning [houses] lit up the heavens. . . . I could stand out on the verandah and for two or three miles watch [the Yankees] as they came on. I could mark when they reached the residence of each and every friend on the road.

Altogether, the Union troops caused an estimated one hundred million dollars' worth of damage in a path carved sixty miles wide through the state. On December 22, 1864, they reached the Georgia coast. "I beg to present you," Sherman wrote to the president, "as a Christmas gift, the city of Savannah."

The Siege of Petersburg

Grant's plan of conquest included another vital element: stopping Robert E. Lee's Army of Northern Virginia. He had assigned that job to the Army of the Potomac, and he traveled with the troops as they advanced on Richmond. In the spring of 1864, Lee and Grant fought several battles, with terrible losses on both sides. In June the Yankees circled behind the Confederate capital and closed in on Petersburg, a few miles to the south. When Union assaults on the city failed, Grant's weary army dug in for a siege.

Through the summer and into the fall, the men in the trenches braved the blazing sun, drenching rain, and artillery and sharpshooter fire. "So many men were daily struck in the camp and trenches," wrote a Union soldier, "that men became utterly reckless, passing about where balls were striking as though it was their normal life and making a joke of a narrow escape or a noisy whistling ball." The rebels, too, grew reckless in the face of constant enemy fire. "The mortars are thrown up a great height and fall down in the trenches like throwing a ball over a house," wrote an Alabama man in Petersburg. "We have become very perfect in dodging them and unless they are thrown too thick I think I can always escape them."

In September Grant fired a salute from every gun bearing down on Petersburg, in honor of Sherman's capture of Atlanta. Six weeks later, he fired a second victory volley, for Sheridan's defeat of the last Confederate force defending the Shenandoah Valley. November brought the presidential election, and the first time ever that soldiers on active duty could cast their votes. Lincoln's Democratic rival was General George B. McClellan, running on a peace platform. The Union soldiers still admired their old commander, and no one was sure which way they would vote. In the end the troops overwhelmingly supported Lincoln, ensuring his reelection.

Inside Petersburg the Confederates heard the news. Hunkering down in their trenches, they grimly awaited "the renewal of the mortal conflict. The conviction everywhere prevailed," wrote a captain from South Carolina, "that we could sustain but one more campaign."

Final Days

"The soldiers are badly out of heart," reported a Georgia man in January 1865, "for they have been a suffering for nearly four long years and there is no prospect of doing better." The new year found the Confederate army in tatters, many of its men barefooted. Years of fighting on meager rations, along with the recent string of losses and news of hunger and hardships back home, had led to a general sense of depression and hopelessness. Hundreds of men were deserting every day. Like rebel soldier James Baker, they were "not a gone to stay in the field any longer" for they had "fout longe a nuff."

In February 1865 General Sherman's army marched north from Savannah, Georgia, on a path toward Richmond. The Union troops swept "like a full developed cyclone," reported one Confederate officer, "leaving behind . . . a track of desolation and ashes." The damage was especially bad in South Carolina, birthplace of the rebellion. In "that nestingplace of traitors," wrote Samuel Duncan of New Hampshire, "the vengeance which our wartorn veterans have been nursing . . . vented itself to the full." The men "blackened a path 100 miles in width" and left the state's capital, Columbia, in flames.

Prisoners of War

In early 1865 the Union and the Confederacy revived the system of prisoner exchanges that had been halted two years earlier. The condition of the freed prisoners was shocking. No one had expected such a long war, and neither side had made adequate arrangements for housing large numbers of captives. Converted factories or warehouses and hastily built stockades served as prisons. They were filthy, overcrowded, and critically short of food, shelter, and medical care. Altogether, about 400,000 men passed through prison camps in the North and South, and more than 50,000 died of disease, malnutrition, exposure, or despair.

The worst camp was Andersonville, in southwest Georgia. This immense open stockade was meant for 10,000 prisoners but held more than 30,000. The men crowded together in crude shelters made of scrap wood, tent fragments, or blankets stretched over holes in the ground. Their only water came from an ankle-deep stream that doubled as a sewer. Daily rations consisted of $1\frac{1}{4}$ pounds of cornmeal and either 1 pound of beef or $\frac{1}{3}$ pound of bacon, often too spoiled to eat. When Lucius Barber of Illinois first arrived at the "Georgia Hell," he could hardly believe that the inmates were human beings. "Hunger, sickness, exposure and dirt had so transformed them," he recalled, "that they more resembled walking skeletons, painted black. . . . Such squalid, filthy wretchedness, hunger, disease, nakedness and cold, I never saw before."

Nearly 13,000 Union soldiers died at the infamous Confederate prison camp Andersonville.

In besieged Petersburg, Lee's army had shrunk to 35,000, facing an opposing force of 125,000 arrayed in a huge semicircle more than fifty miles long. Grant ordered an all-out assault on the center of the rebel lines. On April 2 Lee abandoned the city, sending Jefferson Davis an urgent message: "My lines are broken in three places. Richmond must be evacuated this evening."

Surrender at Appomattox

As the Confederates fled their capital, the Army of Northern Virginia marched west, with Union troops on its heels. The men were "fighting all day, marching all night," wrote Southern general John B. Gordon, commander of the rear guard.

> On and on, hour after hour, from hilltop to hilltop, the lines were alternately forming, fighting and retreating, making one almost continuous shifting battle. . . . The roads and fields swarmed with the eager pursuers.

Confederates retreating from Richmond, Virginia, on April 2, 1865, set much of the city on fire, destroying nearly one thousand buildings. "We are under the shadow of ruins," a newspaperman wrote the next day. "The wreck, the loneliness, seem interminable."

No rations were issued. The hungry Confederates staggered on, eating the dried corn meant for the horses and drinking from rivers and springs. Near the village of Appomattox Court House, Virginia, they found themselves almost completely surrounded, outnumbered four to one. On April 9 General Lee sent a messenger bearing a white flag to General Grant. The two commanders met in the parlor of a private home, where Lee surrendered his army.

Afterward, the Confederate general rode back to camp with "his head . . . sunk low on his breast." The road filled with his soldiers. Some cheered, recalled a rebel officer, some "looked upon him with swimming eyes," and a few battle-hardened veterans "covered their faces with their hands, and wept like children."

Elisha Hunt Rhodes, now commanding officer of his Rhode Island regiment, was in the Union camp, nervously awaiting news of the surrender. Suddenly a soldier

> rode like mad down the road with hat off shouting: "The war is over and we are going home!" . . . The men threw their knapsacks and canteens into the air and howled like mad. . . . I cried and laughed by turns. I never was so happy in my life. . . . Thank God it is over and that the Union is restored.

AT THE CIVIL WAR'S END, A HARD ROAD STILL LAY AHEAD FOR BLACK AMERICANS. SLAVERY WAS DEAD. (IT WOULD BE OFFICIALLY ABOLISHED IN DECEMBER 1865 WITH THE THIRTEENTH AMENDMENT TO THE CONSTITUTION.) THE STRUGGLE FOR CIVIL RIGHTS AND TRUE FREEDOM, HOWEVER, HAD JUST BEGUN. FOR THE TIME BEING, MILLIONS OF AFRICAN AMERICANS JOYFULLY CELEBRATED THE UNION VICTORY. A FEW FREED SLAVES EVEN GOT A CHANCE TO HAVE THE LAST WORD WITH THEIR FORMER MASTERS.

Dayton, Ohio, August 7, 1865

To my old Master, Colonel P. H. Anderson, Big Spring, Tenn.
Sir: I got your letter, and was glad to find that you had not forgotten Jourdon, and that you wanted me to come back and live with you again, promising to do better for me than anybody else can. I have often felt uneasy about you. I thought the Yankees would have hung you long before [this], for harboring Rebs they found at your house. I suppose they

never heard about your going to Colonel Martin's to kill the Union soldier that was left by his company in their stable. Although you shot at me twice before I left you, I did not want to hear of your being hurt, and am glad you are still living. . . .

I want to know particularly what the good chance is you propose to give me. I am doing tolerably well here. I get twenty-five dollars a month, with victuals [food] and clothing; have a comfortable home for Mandy—the folks call her Mrs. Anderson—and the children. . . .

As to my freedom, which you say I can have, there is nothing to be gained on that score, as I got my free papers in 1864. . . . Mandy says she would be afraid to go back without some proof that you were disposed to treat us justly and kindly; and we have concluded to test your sincerity by asking you to send us our wages for the time we served you. This will make us forget and forgive old scores, and rely on your justice and friendship in the future. I served you faithfully for thirty-two years, and Mandy twenty years. At twenty-five dollars a month for me, and two dollars a week for Mandy, our earnings would amount to eleven thousand six hundred and eighty dollars. Add to this the interest for the time our wages have been kept back, and deduct what you paid for our clothing, and three doctor's visits to me, and pulling a tooth for Mandy, and the balance will show what we are in justice entitled to. . . . We trust the good Maker has opened your eyes to the wrongs which you and your fathers have done to me and my fathers, in making us toil for you for generations without recompense. Here I draw my wages every Saturday night; but in Tennessee there was never any pay-day for the Negroes any more than for the horses and cows. . . .

Say howdy to George Carter, and thank him for taking the pistol from you when you were shooting at me.

From your old servant,
Jourdon Anderson

Conclusion

"Touched with Fire"

In the weeks after the surrender at Appomattox, the remaining Confederate forces laid down their arms. Four long years of fighting were over. The war had claimed more than 620,000 lives—one out of every five men who fought. One of the last casualties was President Lincoln, who was assassinated on April 14, 1865, by fanatical pro-Confederate actor John Wilkes Booth.

The surviving soldiers went home and tried to pick up the pieces of their old lives. In the South they found poverty and incredible devastation. Farms and factories had been burned, railroads destroyed, whole towns and even counties evacuated. It would take many years for hardworking Southerners to recover and rebuild. During that process, black Americans would suffer as the "old slaveholding spirit" was reborn in a system of segregation and discrimination that denied them the rights for which so many had died.

The North had largely escaped physical damage. Even so, Union soldiers often found their homecoming difficult. Many felt a vague but persistent discontent. Having lived through the larger-than-life drama of battle, "they were not satisfied," observed Ulysses S. Grant, "with the farm, the store, or the workshop of the villages, but wanted larger fields." Thousands of these restless young men would seek new adventures in the lands opening up in the Far West.

Veterans on both sides also brooded over the meaning of the terrible conflict. So much had been lost and so much changed. After all the killing and destruction, suffering and heartache, the United States was a different nation. Slavery had been destroyed, along with a whole way of life based on it. Secession had been laid to rest and the idea of one united, indivisible nation had risen firmly in its place. "Great rights, great interests, great systems of habit and of thought disappear," said a *New York Times* editorial in 1867. "It leaves us a different people in everything."

In 1913, on the fiftieth anniversary of the Battle of Gettysburg, the federal government held a reunion. Gray-haired survivors of the Union and Confederate forces camped on the old battlefield. They shared memories of a time when, as one

Civil War veterans reenact Pickett's Charge, at the fiftieth-anniversary reunion at Gettysburg in 1913.

veteran put it, their hearts were "touched with fire." The reunion's most dramatic moment was a reenactment of Pickett's Charge. As the thin line of Confederates crossed the field, bearing canes and umbrellas in place of muskets, they broke into the old rebel yell. "After half a century of silence," wrote a photographer, the Union veterans responded with

> a moan, a sigh, a gigantic gasp of unbelief. . . . It was then that the Yankees, unable to restrain themselves longer, burst from behind the stone wall, and flung themselves upon their former enemies . . . not in mortal combat, but re-united in brotherly love and affection.

Time Line of Civil War Events

1860

NOVEMBER 6
Abraham Lincoln is elected sixteenth U.S. president.

DECEMBER 20
South Carolina secedes from the Union. Within two months six other Southern states will follow: Mississippi, Florida, Alabama, Georgia, Louisiana, and Texas.

1861

FEBRUARY 9
Delegates from the seven seceded states meet in Montgomery, Alabama, to form the Confederate States of America, with former U.S. senator Jefferson Davis of Mississippi as president.

APRIL 12
Confederate guns open fire on Fort Sumter in Charleston, South Carolina, beginning the Civil War.

APRIL 15
Lincoln issues a proclamation calling for 75,000 state militiamen.

APRIL 17
Virginia secedes from the Union. Within five weeks Arkansas, Tennessee, and North Carolina will follow, forming an eleven-state Confederacy.

APRIL 19
Lincoln orders a blockade of all Southern ports.

APRIL 20
Robert E. Lee resigns his commission in the U.S. Army and accepts command of Virginia's forces.

MAY 20
Richmond, Virginia, is named the new Confederate capital.

JULY 21
First Battle of Bull Run (Manassas): Confederate forces under General Thomas "Stonewall" Jackson defeat the Union army under General Irvin McDowell at Manassas, Virginia.

1862

MARCH 8–9
The Confederate *Merrimack* and Union *Monitor* engage in the world's first battle between ironclad ships.

MARCH 17
General George B. McClellan and the Army of the Potomac begin an unsuccessful five-month drive to capture Richmond.

APRIL 6–7
Battle of Shiloh (Pittsburg Landing): Confederate troops mount a surprise attack on General Ulysses S. Grant's forces at Shiloh on the Tennessee River. Some 23,000 men are killed, wounded, or missing.

APRIL 16
The Confederate Congress enacts the first military draft in American history.

APRIL 29
A Union navy fleet under David Farragut captures New Orleans.

AUGUST 29–30
Second Battle of Bull Run (Manassas): 55,000 Confederates commanded by Stonewall Jackson and James Longstreet defeat 75,000 Union troops under General John Pope.

SEPTEMBER 17
Battle of Antietam (Sharpsburg): Lee and the Confederates are halted at Antietam Creek in Sharpsburg, Maryland, in the bloodiest day of the war, with 26,000 casualties.

SEPTEMBER 22
Lincoln issues the Emancipation Proclamation, freeing all slaves in territories held by the Confederates.

DECEMBER 13
Union forces under General Ambrose Burnside make a failed assault on Confederates in fortified positions overlooking Fredericksburg, Virginia.

1863

JANUARY 1
The Emancipation Proclamation takes effect.

MARCH 3
The U.S. Congress passes the Enrollment Act of 1863.

MAY 1–4
47,000 Confederates under Lee defeat 70,000 Union troops under General Joseph Hooker at Chancellorsville, Virginia.

MAY 27
The Union stages a failed attack on Port Hudson, Louisiana, in the first major battle involving black troops.

JUNE 3
Lee leads 75,000 Confederate soldiers in an invasion of the North.

1863

JUNE 7
Union troops beat back a Confederate attack at Milliken's Bend, Louisiana.

JULY 1–3
Battle of Gettysburg: 51,000 are killed, wounded, or missing in three days of fighting at Gettysburg, Pennsylvania; the last major Confederate offensive of the war.

JULY 4
Vicksburg, Mississippi, surrenders after a six-week siege by Union forces under General Grant.

JULY 18
The Fifty-fourth Massachusetts Volunteer Infantry leads an attack on Fort Wagner, South Carolina.

SEPTEMBER 19–20
The Confederates defeat the Yankees on Chickamauga Creek, twelve miles below Chattanooga, Tennessee, in the bloodiest battle in the West.

NOVEMBER 19
Lincoln delivers the Gettysburg Address at a ceremony dedicating the battlefield as a national cemetery.

1864

MARCH 2
Grant becomes general in chief of all Union armies.

APRIL 12
Confederate forces under General Nathan Bedford Forrest capture Fort Pillow in Tennessee, slaughtering hundreds of surrendering Union troops, especially blacks.

MAY 8–19
Battle of Spotsylvania Court House: More than 20,000 troops under Generals Grant and Lee are lost in twelve days of fighting in a Virginia town on the road to Richmond.

JUNE 12
Grant begins a campaign to capture Petersburg, Virginia.

AUGUST 5
A Union fleet under David Farragut captures Mobile, Alabama.

1865

SEPTEMBER 2
Union forces under General William T. Sherman capture Atlanta, Georgia.

NOVEMBER 8
Lincoln is reelected president.

NOVEMBER 16
Sherman's army begins a month-long march from Atlanta to Savannah, Georgia, destroying everything in its path.

JANUARY 31
Congress passes the Thirteenth Amendment to the U.S. Constitution, abolishing slavery.

APRIL 2
Confederate troops abandon the defense of Petersburg, and Richmond is evacuated.

APRIL 3
Richmond surrenders to Union forces.

APRIL 9
Lee surrenders to Grant at Appomattox Court House, Virginia.

APRIL 14
Lincoln is assassinated by John Wilkes Booth at Ford's Theatre in Washington, D.C. The next morning Vice President Andrew Johnson assumes the presidency.

DECEMBER 6
The Thirteenth Amendment is ratified by the states.

Glossary

abolitionist A person in favor of abolishing, or putting an end to, slavery.

arsenal A place used for the manufacturing or storage of weapons and other military equipment.

blockade The act of blocking enemy ports to prevent imports and exports.

blockade runners Fast Confederate ships, usually camouflaged with gray paint, that were used to slip through the Union blockade, smuggling war materials and luxury goods into the South and smuggling out cotton.

boatswain A naval officer in charge of a ship's hull and related equipment.

border states The slaveholding states on the border between North and South, which included Delaware, Kentucky, Maryland, Missouri, and Virginia. Only Virginia joined the Confederacy; the western part of the state declared its independence and joined the Union as West Virginia.

grapeshot Clusters of small iron balls shot from a cannon.

plantation A large farm estate; in Civil War times, a large Southern farm worked by slaves.

secession The act of seceding, or formally withdrawing, from a group or an organization.

siege The surrounding of a fort or city, in which the attackers cut off food and other supplies to force the enemy to surrender.

teamster Someone who drives a team of horses, mules, or other draft animals.

Underground Railroad A secret network of abolitionists who fed, sheltered, and guided runaway slaves on their journey north to freedom.

To Find Out More

BOOKS

Dudley, William, ed. *The Civil War: Opposing Viewpoints.* San Diego: Greenhaven Press, 1995.
A selection of speeches, articles, and other primary sources that present opposing views on the issues of the day, including slavery, secession, war strategies, and African-American enlistment.

Golay, Michael. *The Civil War.* America at War series. New York: Facts on File, 1992.
A clear and interesting account of the background and key battles of the war.

McPherson, James M. *For Cause & Comrades: Why Men Fought in the Civil War.* New York: Oxford University Press, 1997.
————. *What They Fought For, 1861–1865.* Baton Rouge, LA: Louisiana State University Press, 1994.
Both of these books by Pulitzer Prize-winning historian McPherson draw on the letters and diaries of Union and Confederate soldiers to examine what led men to risk their lives fighting the Civil War. **For Cause & Comrades** *is a longer and more detailed study.*

Meltzer, Milton. *Voices from the Civil War: A Documentary History of the Great American Conflict.* New York: Thomas Y. Crowell, 1989.
A varied, entertaining collection of letters, diaries, songs, and other personal writings by both soldiers and civilians, connected by a running history of the major events and issues of the war.

Mettger, Zak. *Till Victory Is Won: Black Soldiers in the Civil War.* New York: Puffin, 1994.
First-person accounts and lots of black-and-white photographs bring alive the story of the challenges and contributions of African-American soldiers in the Civil War.

Schomp, Virginia. *The Civil War.* New York: Benchmark Books, 2002.
Companion volume in the LETTERS FROM THE HOMEFRONT *series.*

————. *He Fought for Freedom: Frederick Douglass.* New York: Marshall Cavendish, 1997.
Benchmark Biography of the great African-American abolitionist, writer, and newspaper publisher.

ON THE INTERNET*

"AmericanCivilWar.com" at http://americancivilwar.com
Designed for students of all ages, this site offers a wealth of information on Civil War battles, historical background, documents, political leaders, black troops, women in the war, and much more.

"American Memory, Library of Congress: Selected Civil War Photographs Collection" at http://memory.loc.gov/ammem/cwphtml/cwphome.html
More than a thousand Civil War photographs from the Library of Congress collection, including portraits, battle preparations, and after-battle scenes.

"Civil War Battles by State" at http://www.americancivilwar.com/statepic/ index.html
This site offers state-by-state maps and descriptions of Civil War battles, along with a time line, key documents, and biographies of women on both sides of the fight.

"The Civil War for Kids" at http://www2.lhric.org/pocantico/civilwar/cwar.htm
Created by a class of New York elementary school students, this site offers graphs comparing the resources of North and South, drawings of flags and uniforms, activity sheets, and more.

"Civil War in Miniature: A Compendium and Civil War Reference Site" at http://civilwarmini.com
An in-depth site with short stories, art, folklore, battle information, quizzes, puzzles, a time line, maps, photographs, and statistics. Great graphics and music.

"Kid Info: Civil War Reconstruction" at http://www.kidinfo.com/American_History/Civil_War.html
Excellent source of links to Civil War sites. A good first stop for students looking for facts, dates, photographs, biographies, and documents.

*Websites change from time to time. For additional on-line information, check with the media specialist at your local library.

VIDEOS

The Civil War: A Film by Ken Burns. Produced by Ken Burns and Ric Burns. Distributed by Turner Home Entertainment, PBS Home Video, 1997.
Excellent documentary taking the viewer from Fort Sumter through Lincoln's assassination; available on five videos or DVDs.

Civil War Journal: The 54th Massachusetts. A Presentation of the History Channel. Produced by Greystone Communications and A & E Network. Distributed by New Video Group. © 1995 A & E Television Networks.
Fifty-minute documentary on the 54th Massachusetts Volunteer Infantry, the all-black regiment famous for its courageous assault on Fort Wagner, South Carolina.

Bibliography

Alcott, Louisa May. *Hospital Sketches.* Edited by Bessie Z. Jones. Cambridge, MA: Harvard University Press, 1960.

Bacot, Ada W. *A Confederate Nurse: The Diary of Ada W. Bacot, 1860–1863.* Edited by Jean V. Berlin. Columbia, SC: University of South Carolina Press, 1994.

Bowman, John S., ed. *The Civil War Almanac.* New York: World Almanac, 1985.

Burgess, Lauren Cook, ed. *An Uncommon Soldier: The Civil War Letters of Sarah Rosetta Wakeman, Alias Private Lyons Wakeman.* New York: Oxford University Press, 1994.

Callaway, Joshua K. *The Civil War Letters of Joshua K. Callaway.* Edited by Judith Lee Hallock. Athens, GA: University of Georgia Press, 1997.

Carroll, Andrew, ed. *War Letters.* New York: Scribner, 2001.

Catton, Bruce. *The American Heritage New History of the Civil War.* Edited by James M. McPherson. New York: MetroBooks, 2001.

Cornish, Dudley Taylor. *The Sable Arm: Black Troops in the Union Army, 1861–1865.* Lawrence, KS: University Press of Kansas, 1987.

Davis, Kenneth C. *Don't Know Much about the Civil War: Everything You Need to Know about America's Greatest Conflict but Never Learned.* New York: William Morrow, 1996.

Garfield, James A. *The Wild Life of the Army: Civil War Letters of James A. Garfield.* Edited by Frederick D. Williams. East Lansing, MI: Michigan State University Press, 1964.

Golay, Michael. *The Civil War.* New York: Facts on File, 1992.

Gooding, James Henry. *On the Altar of Freedom: A Black Soldier's Civil War Letters from the Front.* Edited by Virginia M. Adams. Amherst, MA: University of Massachusetts Press, 1991.

Higginson, Thomas Wentworth. *Army Life in a Black Regiment.* Boston: Beacon Press, 1962.

Holzer, Harold, ed. *Dear Mr. Lincoln: Letters to the President.* New York: Addison-Wesley, 1993.

Jones, Katharine M. *Heroines of Dixie: Confederate Women Tell Their Story of the War.* New York: Bobbs-Merrill, 1955.

Kent, Zachary. *The Civil War: "A House Divided."* Springfield, NJ: Enslow Publishers, 1994.

McPherson, James M. *For Cause & Comrades: Why Men Fought in the Civil War.* New York: Oxford University Press, 1997.

———. *Marching toward Freedom: Blacks in the Civil War, 1861–1865.* New York: Facts on File, 1991.

———. *The Negro's Civil War: How American Blacks Felt and Acted during the War for the Union.* New York: Ballantine, 1991.

———. *What They Fought For, 1861–1865.* Baton Rouge, LA: Louisiana State University Press, 1994.

Marvel, William, ed. *The* Monitor *Chronicles.* New York: Simon & Schuster, 2000.

Rhodes, Elisha Hunt. *All for the Union: The Civil War Diary and Letters of Elisha Hunt Rhodes.* Edited by Robert Hunt Rhodes. New York: Orion Books, 1991.

Sewell, Richard H. *A House Divided: Sectionalism and Civil War, 1848–1865.* Baltimore: Johns Hopkins University Press, 1988.

Sherman, William Tecumseh. *Memoirs of General W. T. Sherman.* New York: Library of America, 1990.

Silber, Nina, and Mary Beth Sievens. *Yankee Correspondence: Civil War Letters between New England Soldiers and the Home Front.* Charlottesville, VA: University Press of Virginia, 1996.

Spiegel, Marcus M. *A Jewish Colonel in the Civil War.* Edited by Jean Powers Soman and Frank L. Byrne. Lincoln, NE: University of Nebraska Press, 1994.

Strode, Hudson, ed. *Jefferson Davis: Private Letters, 1823–1889.* New York: Harcourt, Brace and World, 1966.

Sullivan, Walter, ed. *The War the Women Lived: Female Voices from the Confederate South.* Nashville: J. S. Sanders, 1995.

Ward, Geoffrey, Ric Burns, and Ken Burns. *The Civil War: An Illustrated History.* New York: Alfred A. Knopf, 1990.

Welsh, Peter. *Irish Green & Union Blue: The Civil War Letters of Peter Welsh.* Edited by Lawrence Frederick Kohl and Margaret Cossé Richard. New York: Fordham University Press, 1986.

Wiley, Bell Irvin. *The Life of Billy Yank: The Common Soldier of the Union.* New York: Charter Books, 1952.

———. *The Life of Johnny Reb: The Common Soldier of the Confederacy.* Baton Rouge, LA: Louisiana State University Press, 1978.

Notes on Quotes

The quotations in this book are from the following sources:

Introduction: America Divided
p. 7, "no peace for the South": Ward and Burns, *Civil War*, p. 5.
p. 7, "declaration of war": Sewell, *House Divided*, p. 78.

Chapter One: Fighting for the Confederacy
p. 8, "The Yankees": diary of John D. Martin, 25th Indiana Volunteers, from E-mail to
  author by Charles Frederick, November 3, 1999.
p. 8, "I never": McPherson, *For Cause & Comrades*, p. 17.
p. 8, "dropped their ledgers": Ward and Burns, *Civil War*, p. 55.
p. 8, "the scum": McPherson, *For Cause & Comrades*, p. 17.
p. 11, "the holy cause": McPherson, *What They Fought For*, p. 11.
p. 11, "If we should": McPherson, *For Cause & Comrades*, p. 21.
p. 11, "We went bowling along": Ward and Burns, *Civil War*, p. 54.
p. 12, "Made my first detail": Wiley, *Johnny Reb*, p. 27.
p. 15, "The boys were saying": ibid., pp. 66–67.
p. 15, "yell like furies!": ibid., p. 67.
p. 16, "those Yankees": ibid., p. 120.
p. 16, "a sort of": Ward and Burns, *Civil War*, p. 267.
p. 16, "this side": ibid., p. 67.
p. 17, "A more oppressive law": Wiley, *Johnny Reb*, p. 130.
p. 17, "This is a Rich": McPherson, *For Cause & Comrades*, p. 102.
p. 20, "like sheep": Ward and Burns, *Civil War*, p. 159.
p. 20, "every stalk of corn": ibid., p. 154.

p. 20, "Our army is": Wiley, *Johnny Reb,* p. 93.

p. 22, "The edge of the conflict": Ward and Burns, *Civil War,* p. 220.

p. 22, "the balls were whizzing": ibid., p. 224.

p. 22, "bayonet thrusts": ibid., p. 232.

p. 23, "Many of us": Meltzer, *Voices,* p. 102.

Chapter Two: All for the Union

p. 24, "The soldiers' fare": Wiley, *Billy Yank,* p. 224.

p. 24, "War! and volunteers": ibid., p. 19.

p. 25, "Thousands went forth": McPherson, *What They Fought For,* p. 29.

p. 27, "Union never could": Silber and Sievens, *Yankee Correspondence,* p. 75.

p. 27, "accursed institution": Spiegel, *Jewish Colonel,* p. 316.

p. 27, "I believe that Slavery": McPherson, *For Cause & Comrades,* p. 118.

p. 27, "volunteered to fight": ibid., pp. 122–123.

p. 27, "I have always": ibid., p. 125.

p. 28, "Nothing but drill": Rhodes, *All for the Union,* p. 41.

p. 28, "a well-meaning baboon": Ward and Burns, *Civil War,* p. 75.

p. 28, "This morning": Rhodes, *All for the Union,* p. 79.

p. 29, "certain destruction": Ward and Burns, *Civil War,* p. 203.

p. 30, "Food is scarce": Rhodes, *All for the Union,* p. 65.

p. 30, "A poor man's life": Wiley, *Billy Yank,* p. 282.

p. 30, "I have nothing": ibid., p. 280.

p. 31, "Today we have news": ibid., p. 283.

p. 31, "I saw an open field": Davis, *Don't Know Much,* p. 227.

p. 31, "I can't spare": Bowman, *Civil War Almanac,* p. 339.

p. 31, "the key": Ward and Burns, *Civil War,* p. 212.

p. 34, "Every day" and "favorite amusement": ibid., p. 238.

p. 34, "often talk": Carroll, *War Letters,* pp. 87–88.

p. 35, "grand spectacle": ibid., p. 89.

Chapter Three: Black Troops Fight for Freedom

p. 36, "Once let the black man": "History of African Americans in the Civil War" at http://www.itd.nps.gov/cwss/history/aa_cw_history.htm

p. 37, "in aid of the rebellion": McPherson, *Marching toward Freedom,* p. 17.

p. 39, "teamsters and cooks": McPherson, *For Cause & Comrades,* p. 119.

p. 40, "a contest between": ibid., p. 121.

p. 40, "This is a white": McPherson, *Marching toward Freedom,* p. 6.

p. 40, "We think we are": McPherson, *Negro's Civil War,* p. 165.

p. 40, "[It is] no disgrace": McPherson, *For Cause & Comrades,* p. 127.

p. 41, "persons of color": Catton, *American Heritage,* p. 164.

p. 41, "stepped forward": McPherson, *Negro's Civil War,* p. 159.

p. 42, "Instead of the musket": Holzer, *Dear Mrs. Lincoln*, p. 166.

p. 42, "We are men": Gooding, *On the Altar of Freedom*, p. 49.

p. 42, "We met the foe": ibid.

p. 43, "It is not too much": McPherson, *Negro's Civil War*, p. 195.

p. 44, "golden opportunity": Ward and Burns, *Civil War*, p. 252.

p. 45, "were perfectly exasperated": Golay, *Civil War*, p. 91.

p. 45, "for every soldier": Cornish, *Sable Arm*, p. 168.

p. 45, "The river was dyed": Bowman, *Civil War Almanac*, p. 193.

p. 45, "fought with ropes": Higginson, *Army Life*, p. 251.

p. 45, "not as much afraid": McPherson, *Negro's Civil War*, p. 226.

Chapter Four: Women at the Front

p. 47, "I saw, crowded": Ward and Burns, *Civil War*, p. 298.

p. 48, "Almost every house": Kent, *Civil War*, p. 74.

p. 49, "Nothing that I": Jones, *Heroines of Dixie*, p. 108.

p. 49, "lying all over": ibid., p. 110.

p. 49, "never seen": ibid., p. 108.

p. 49, "determined to make": Alcott, *Hospital Sketches*, p. xxxix.

p. 51, "Tis hard": Bacot, *Confederate Nurse*, p. 119.

p. 51, "while the shells": Kent, *Civil War*, p. 76.

p. 51, "I have never": Davis, *Don't Know Much*, p. 363.

p. 52, "almost irresistible": Catton, *American Heritage*, p. 462.

p. 52, "I had no reason": Jones, *Heroines of Dixie*, p. 65.

p. 54, "This is the only": "Women's History: Harriet Tubman" at
    http://womenshistory.about.com/library/weekly/aa020419c.htm

p. 55, "a mere boy": "24th Regiment, Mississippi Infantry Volunteers, CSA" at
    http://www.mississippiscv.org/MS_Units/24th_MS_INF.htm

p. 55, "only fourteen": Wiley, *Billy Yank*, pp. 300–301.

p. 56, "I am naturally": "Sarah Emma Edmonds" at http://www.civilwarhome.com/
    edmondsbio.htm

p. 56, "do something": Holzer, *Dear Mr. Lincoln*, p. 270.

p. 56, "We discovered": Wiley, *Billy Yank*, p. 339.

Chapter Five: "Desolation and Ashes"

p. 58, "If anyone had": Wiley, *Johnny Reb*, p. 148.

p. 58, "I gave up": Sewell, *House Divided*, p. 151.

p. 61, "get into the interior": Sherman, *Memoirs*, p. 490.

p. 63, "constant roaring": Jones, *Heroines of Dixie*, p. 329.

p. 63, "Atlanta is ours": Bowman, *Civil War Almanac*, p. 221.

p. 63, "crows flying": Ward and Burns, *Civil War*, p. 332.

p. 63, "left nothing": Golay, *Civil War*, p. 162.

p. 64, "appalling and heart-rending": Sherman, *Memoirs,* p. 598.

p. 65, "This is probably": Ward and Burns, *Civil War,* p. 342.

p. 65, "the lurid flames": ibid., p. 343.

p. 65, "I beg to present": ibid., p. 348.

p. 65, "So many men": ibid., p. 308.

p. 65, "The mortars": Wiley, *Johnny Reb,* p. 79.

p. 66, "The renewal": Ward and Burns, *Civil War,* p. 334.

p. 66, "The soldiers" and "not a gone": Wiley, *Johnny Reb,* p. 134.

p. 66, "like a full developed": Sewell, *House Divided,* p. 159.

p. 66, "that nestingplace": Silber and Sievens, *Yankee Correspondence,* p. 51.

p. 67, "Georgia Hell": Davis, *Don't Know Much,* p. 353.

p. 68, "My lines are broken": Ward and Burns, *Civil War,* p. 368.

p. 68, "fighting all day": Davis, *Don't Know Much,* pp. 401–402.

p. 69, "his head": Ward and Burns, *Civil War,* p. 381.

p. 69, "rode like mad": Rhodes, *All for the Union,* pp. 230, 248.

Conclusion: "Touched with Fire"

p. 71, "old slaveholding spirit": *Davis, Don't Know Much,* p. 429.

p. 71, "they were not satisfied": Ward and Burns, *Civil War,* p. 404.

p. 72, "Great rights": ibid., p. 400.

p. 73, "touched with fire": Golay, *Civil War,* p. 172.

p. 73, "After half a century": Ward and Burns, *Civil War,* p. 412.

Acknowledgments

Every effort has been made to trace the copyright holders of the letters reprinted in this book. We apologize for any omissions or errors in this regard and would be pleased to make the appropriate acknowledgments in any future printings.

Grateful acknowledgments are made to the following historical societies, museums, libraries, publishers, and individuals for permission to reprint these materials:

Jefferson Davis to Varina Davis, February 20, 1861. Courtesy of the Museum of the Confederacy, Richmond, Virginia.

Sidney Lanier to Cliff Lanier, December 1861, from Anderson, Charles R., and Aubrey H. Starke, eds., *Letters 1857–1868,* vol. 7 of *The Centennial Edition of the Works of Sidney Lanier,* Baltimore: Johns Hopkins University Press, 1945.

Luke R. Roberts to Mrs. C. M. Roberts, March 28, 1862, Harrisburg Civil War Round Table Collection, Luke R. Roberts Papers. Courtesy of the U.S. Army Military History Institute.

George E. Pickett to La Salle Corbell, July 6, 1863, from Pickett, George E., *The Heart of a Soldier: As Revealed in the Intimate Letters of Genl. George E. Pickett C.S.A.,* New York: Seth Moyle, 1913.

Peter Welsh to Margaret Welsh, February 3, 1863. Courtesy of the New-York Historical Society.

James A. Garfield to Lucretia Garfield, June 14, 1862; and Lewis Douglass to Amelia Loguen, July 20, 1863. Courtesy of the Library of Congress.

George S. Geer to Martha Geer, May 20, 1862. Courtesy of the Mariners' Museum, Newport News, Virginia.

John Boston to Elizabeth Boston, January 12, 1862; and Spotswood Rice to Kittey Diggs, September 3, 1864. Courtesy of the National Archives and Records Administration.

Louisa May Alcott narrative, from Alcott, Louisa May, *Hospital Sketches,* at http://digital.library.upenn.edu/women/alcott/sketches/sketches.html

Belle Boyd narrative, from Boyd, Belle, *Belle Boyd: In Camp and Prison,* London: Saunders, Otley and Company, 1865.

Rosetta Wakeman to her parents, June 5, 1863, from Burgess, Lauren Cook, *An Uncommon Soldier: The Civil War Letters of Sarah Rosetta Wakeman, Alias Pvt. Lyons Wakeman,* New York: Oxford University Press, 1994. Reprinted by permission of the Minerva Center, Pasadena, Maryland.

Joshua K. Callaway to Dulcinea B. Callaway, September 24, 1863, from Callaway, Joshua K., *The Civil War Letters of Joshua K. Callaway,* edited by Judith Lee Hallock, Athens, GA: University of Georgia Press, 1997. Reprinted by permission of the University of Georgia Press.

William T. Sherman to James M. Calhoun, E. E. Rawson, and S. C. Wells, September 12, 1864, from Sherman, William T., *Memoirs of General William T. Sherman: Written by Himself,* New York: D. Appleton & Co., 1875.

Jourdon Anderson to P. H. Anderson, August 7, 1865, from Child, L. Maria, ed., *The Freedmen's Book,* Boston: Ticknor & Fields, 1865.

Index

Page numbers for illustrations are in boldface

About the Author

"After researching and writing books for the *Letters from the Homefront* series, it was fascinating to take a look at America's wars from a different point of view in *Letters from the Battlefront.* While I read the letters, diaries, and reflections of soldiers from the American Revolution all the way through the Vietnam War, I was struck once again by the way, in our fast-changing world, people themselves remain so little changed. The Continental soldier shivering at Valley Forge and the army infantryman in the jungles of South Vietnam wore different uniforms and carried different weapons. They  sometimes used different words to express their feelings. But beneath the skin, their basic concerns and emotions—their love of life, their longing for home and family, their search for meaning amid the bewildering inhumanity of war—were startlingly similar."

VIRGINIA SCHOMP has written more than forty books on nonfiction topics including ancient cultures and American history. Ms. Schomp lives in the Catskill Mountain region of New York with her husband, Richard, and their son, Chip.